LOUISVILLE'S
ALMA KELLNER
—MYSTERY—

LOUISVILLE'S ALMA KELLNER MYSTERY

SHAWN M. HERRON

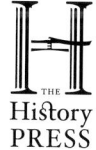

Published by The History Press
Charleston, SC
www.historypress.net

Copyright © 2018 by Shawn M. Herron
All rights reserved

Front cover, top left: Courier-Journal; *top right*: Courier-Journal; *bottom left*: Courier-Journal; *bottom right*: Reno Gazette Journal.
Back cover, top: San Francisco Call; *middle*: Courier-Journal; *bottom*: Courier-Journal.

First published 2018

Manufactured in the United States

ISBN 9781467138161

Library of Congress Control Number: 2017958381

Notice: The information in this book is true and complete to the best of our knowledge. It is offered without guarantee on the part of the author or The History Press. The author and The History Press disclaim all liability in connection with the use of this book.

All rights reserved. No part of this book may be reproduced or transmitted in any form whatsoever without prior written permission from the publisher except in the case of brief quotations embodied in critical articles and reviews.

*To my parents, Eugene and Regenia Herron,
who always believed I could do anything I wanted.*

Contents

Preface	9
Acknowledgements	11
Introduction: A Lonely Grave	13
1. The Crime	15
2. The Search	20
3. The Investigation	26
4. The Discovery	30
5. The Preliminaries	43
6. The Dragnet	61
7. The Capture	66
8. The Writ	84
9. The Arrival	93
10. The Pretrial	99
11. The Trial	105
12. The Appeal	136
13. The Prison	141
14. The Parole	147
15. The Priest	154
Epilogue	157
Notes	163
Bibliography	167
About the Author	173

Preface

Language use at the time of the events depicted in this book differed to some extent than it does today. For example, the words *street*, *avenue* and *pike* used in an address were printed in lowercase, and that convention will be followed here.

Certain words were not spelled as they are today; except in quotes, the modern spelling will be used. The use of the word *clew* (clue) is one example.

The names of many of the individuals involved in this crime have varied spellings in the news accounts. To the extent possible, I have standardized these to the spelling most commonly used, but I have not changed the spelling in direct quotes.

Acknowledgements

When I first came across this story, I became intrigued, as I have worked many missing persons cases over the years. A long-missing child is the ultimate horror for a family, of course. As I learned more about this story, I realized how complex it was and how much could be learned—even today—and applied to similar cases.

During the research and writing process, I have had more support than I can fully describe. Much appreciation is extended to the library resources and staff of the Louisville Free Public Library and the University of Louisville, Brandeis School of Law, Law Library, who pointed me in the right direction. Online resources used include, but are certainly not limited to, Newspapers.com and Ancestry.com, which I used to chase down details of family relationships. Although of course the *Courier-Journal* and the *Louisville Times* were the primary sources of information on the case, other newspapers in cities across the nation also contributed to the telling of the story. Unless otherwise noted, all images are courtesy of the *Courier-Journal*.

The most tremendous and unique source of information, however, was the transcript of the original trial, located purely by happenstance at the University of Notre Dame Library.

Family, friends and coworkers kept me bolstered throughout: my mom—and my dad, in spirit—of course; my cousins Peggy and Debbie; friends Gail, Robert and Brenda; and so many others I can't begin to name. The encouragement I received gave me the incentive to finish this story.

Introduction
A Lonely Grave

In December 1909, Louisville citizens were mystified by the sudden disappearance of eight-year-old Alma Kellner, stolen away, apparently, during her devotions after Mass. Residents were then horrified by the discovery of her body, almost six months later, just one hundred yards from where she was last seen. The ghastly murder of this young girl galvanized the nation—and the world—as a manhunt took a determined Louisville police detective thousands of miles across the country in search of his murderous quarry.

The discovery of young Alma's body coincided with the dedication of Kentucky's new capitol building, and the governor would take time from the festivities to perform his own grim duties related to the investigation. At the same time that Joseph Wendling was being chased across the country, Dr. Hawley Harvey Crippen, suspected of murdering his wife in England, and his lover were being chased across the ocean. Both men were apprehended within days of each other. The two manhunts dueled for headlines on the front pages of newspapers across the nation and the world. It was a race to learn who would be captured first. Wendling, the accused killer of Alma Kellner, was apprehended in San Francisco only a day before Dr. Hawley Crippen was found in Canada. For a few days in 1910, Louisville residents waited anxiously for the resolution of the trial.

A next generation of Louisville residents, who likely knew of the murder only from their parents, followed the end of the story, with Joseph Wendling boarding a ship to leave the United States and return to France, the place of his birth.

Introduction

Even today, many of the landmarks in this case that gripped the nation and the world for weeks still stand, their significance forgotten. The graves of those involved are scattered throughout Louisville and extend even to other states, many almost certainly never visited by anyone who knows who the interred are. Alma Kellner's grave may perhaps draw the attention of a passerby who wonders why a child died so young. Doubtless, family members of many of the parties still live in Louisville, and they perhaps have no knowledge at all of the roles their family members played in the case. Maybe this story will cause more than one person to pause while passing by the places that formed the backdrop for the events and consider, for just a moment, the layers of history reflected there.

1
THE CRIME

All that can be said, with any degree of certainty, is that on the morning of Wednesday, December 8, 1909, Alma Katherine Kellner, age eight, left her home at 507 East Broadway in Louisville, Kentucky, to attend Mass at St. John's Catholic Church. The church, located at the intersection of Clay street and East Walnut street, now Muhammad Ali Boulevard, was some six blocks from the Kellner residence. Young Alma had walked that route many times before. The church was so close, in fact, that its spires would have been visible from the Kellner home. Alma had attended Mass there just the previous Sunday with a playmate, although the Kellner family, Frederick F. (Fred), Florence and their three children usually attended Mass at St. Boniface's Catholic Church, a few blocks farther north from their home. The neighborhood, then home to generations of descendants of German immigrants, many of the Roman Catholic faith, boasted several churches of various denominations in the immediate area.

According to her maternal aunt, Elizabeth Weitzel, who lived with the Kellners and helped Alma dress that morning, young Alma left for Mass wearing a plaid dress, a "cream tan brown with a little green and an old rose stripe in it." The dress was trimmed with green velvet and had a green velvet collar, pearl buttons and a white guimpe (a high-necked blouse worn under a dress with a lower neckline). It was a bitterly cold morning, so the child was also wearing a black-and-white-checked coat with a velvet collar and an emblem on the arms. Her hat was a mushroom

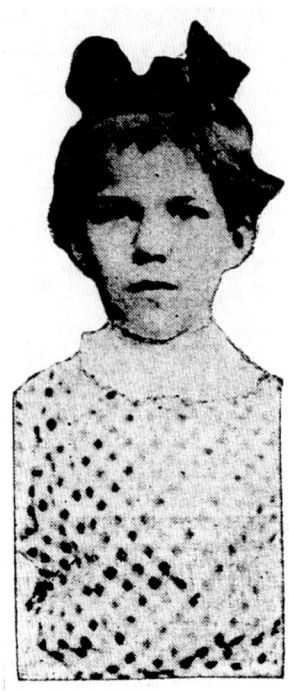

Alma Kellner, as she appeared shortly before her murder, published in the *Courier-Journal*.

shape, a popular style at the time, and was dark red. Her stockings were black-ribbed knit, and under her dress she wore a white-ribbed undershirt and black lingerie. Her gloves were tan, kid, leather gauntlets with a red star. Her buttoned, black shoes were ones she had worn for some time, her aunt having made the decision that Alma should wear her old shoes rather than a new pair she had recently received. She carried a brand-new handkerchief in her coat pocket, made of a crossbar fabric with a small bowknot emblem in the corner. She left the house at approximately 9:45 a.m. for the High Mass celebrating the Feast of the Immaculate Conception of the Virgin Mary, electing to attend the church closer to her home rather than the family's usual parish. (Her mother and aunt had already attended Mass earlier that morning.) Before Alma left the house, she played with her young brother, Frederick Jr. On departing, she kissed her mother and baby brother goodbye. Her mother and her aunt watched her skip east down Broadway.

She walked east and was seen by Dr. W.B.C. Yont, a druggist whose store was located at the northeast corner of Hancock street and Broadway.[1] Dr. Yont initially thought Alma was coming inside. Instead, she simply waved as she passed by and turned north on Hancock street. She was alone at the time. She was also seen by William Augustus, the neighborhood postman walking down the west side of Hancock street just north of Gray street. She also greeted him.

She did not return from Mass as her mother expected at the end of the service, and as her mother had directed her to do. By 11:30 a.m., her mother began to look for her daughter to return and, eventually, became uneasy when Alma did not appear. Others at the house, perhaps her sister, convinced Mrs. Kellner that Alma had simply gone to a friend's home for dinner and would return soon. As the hours passed, however, Mrs. Kellner became "greatly alarmed" and telephoned her husband. Fred Kellner was at work at his family's business, the Frank Fehr Brewing

Company, part of the larger Central Consumers Company. He soon came home, and a search of the area began. Every friend and family member in the area was contacted.

Father George Schumann, the rector of the church, was contacted about Alma's disappearance. He explained that the High Mass that day, celebrating the feast day, had been at 9:00 a.m., rather than at 10:00 a.m., as Alma and her mother had believed. He stated that he had not noticed Alma at Mass that morning. He would have been familiar with her, as she was a third-grade student at the nearby Sisters of Mercy Academy at 1172 East Broadway. Although the parish also had its own elementary school, the priest likely knew Alma, at least by sight, as a child in the neighborhood who almost certainly had friends at the school.[2] Sister Mary Columbia, the superior of Alma's elementary school, began to check with the children she knew Alma was acquainted with, but none had seen her since school ended on Tuesday afternoon. Realizing that Alma had, in fact, really disappeared, Sister Columbia and the other nuns retreated to the chapel to pray for her safe return.

As the day waned and the sun set, Mrs. Kellner became distraught and broke down. The family, thinking Alma may have elected to attend Mass elsewhere when she realized she had missed her intended service, began to call all of the Catholic churches in the area, certainly St. Joseph's, St. Boniface's and St. Martin of Tours, but none of the priests had seen a child matching Alma Kellner's description. Mr. Kellner stated the next morning, as quoted in the *Louisville Courier-Journal*, that "Alma would always know the way home, and if she had gotten lost she would do as we always told her to do, tell her name and address."

He continued:

> *I am convinced that she has either been stolen or suffered an accident that has resulted in her death or serious injury. Where she could be I do not know, but I will leave no stone unturned to find her. She may be in the river, and if she is we will drag the river to find her. I am all but crazy and do not know what to do. I can hardly remain in the house when I know that my baby is away from home, either dead or in the hands of those who are her enemies.*

Finally, the Kellners contacted the Second Police District. The acting night chief of the Louisville Police Department, Captain F.P. Portman, spread the alarm to officers throughout the city. (Although police departments at

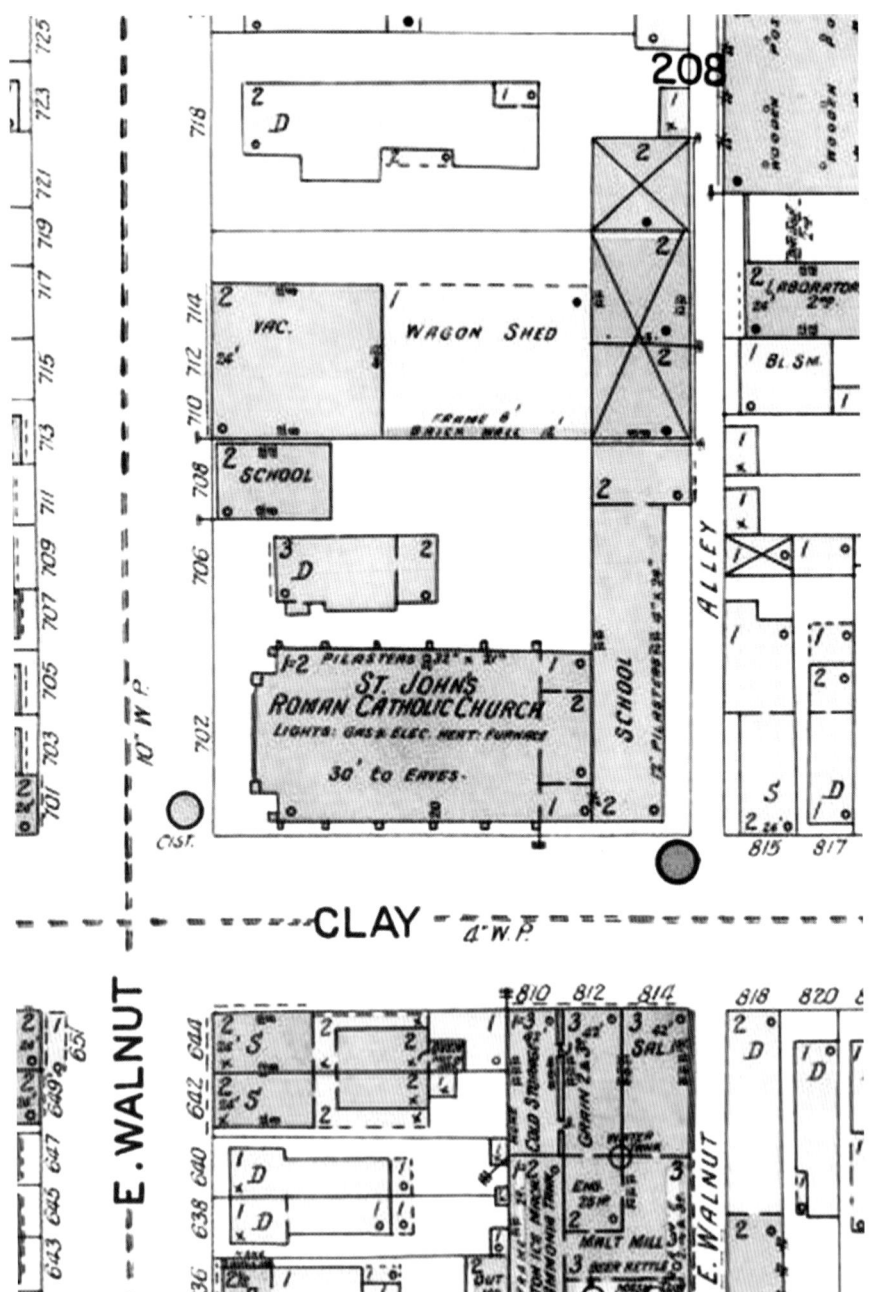

Above: 1905 Sanborn Fire Insurance map of Louisville. *Courtesy of the Sanborn Map Company, Colorado Springs, Colorado.*

Opposite: A photo of Alma Kellner, published in the *Courier-Journal*.

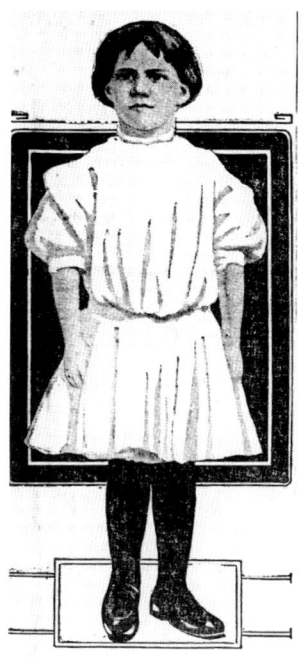

the time lacked radios, all of the stations had telephones and station keepers, and the process of disseminating information was remarkably efficient.) Louisville police officers were directed to investigate every child on the streets and to "arrest all persons who might be suspicious in their actions." Hospitals, doctors and drugstores were also informed, should she have met with an accident. It was recognized quickly by the authorities that Alma was the granddaughter of the late J.F. Kellner, the president of the Central Consumers Company and a wealthy man, leading to speculation that she had been kidnapped and was being held for ransom, although no note or other communication had as yet been received.

Despite all of the efforts, "the child could not be found."

2
THE SEARCH

By the next morning, the first newspaper reports had spread the news to the residents of Louisville. The daily newspapers, both the *Courier-Journal* and the *Louisville Times*, printed photographs of Alma and described her as being about four feet tall, with light brown hair and large blue eyes, and with rosy cheeks. The clothing description indicated that she was wearing a light plaid dress, a black-and-white jacket and a red hat trimmed with a plaid ribbon.

Alma's parents, as would be expected, reportedly did not sleep at all that first night. Mrs. Kellner was so distraught that Dr. T. Hunt Stuckey was summoned the next day to attend to her, presumably to give her a sedative of some type. Given Fred Kellner's position as the general solicitor for the Central Consumers Company, he believed—as did others—that Alma had been kidnapped and was being held for ransom. However, although the Fehr-Kellner family was considered wealthy, and Fred Kellner was mentioned in the will of the recently deceased founder of the company, the estate had not yet been settled. Alma Kellner's parents were considered to be in "good circumstances" but not "especially rich." In addition, Florence Kellner was the daughter of Gabriel Weitzel, a Frankfort innkeeper, also from a middle-class family.

The thought that Alma had been injured accidentally and had been taken for medical care was soon discounted, as no word of an unknown child had come to the police or her family from any hospital or doctor.

The *Courier-Journal* noted this was the "hardest and most serious case with which [the police] have had to contend" for several years, comparing it to a high-profile kidnapping of a young boy in Sharon, Pennsylvania, earlier in the year. Fred Kellner was reportedly holding up very well under the strain and worry and was "personally superintending much of the work of hunting for the girl."

Mrs. Kellner again assured the newspapermen who called on the family that Alma could not be lost, as she was a bright girl who knew the area well and that, even if she was lost, she knew to provide her name and address to an adult for help. The Kellners had lived in the house on Broadway for two years, and Alma had regularly walked to church and to her elementary school, some distance to the east on Broadway, alone. As such, her mother was convinced that Alma had been kidnapped. She exhausted herself with weeping and only then was convinced to lie down and rest.

At the same time, the Louisville police, "baffled at the mysterious disappearance," had investigated through the night, questioning everyone along the route that they could contact. Young Alma was well known on Broadway, as she walked to and from her elementary school regularly, yet no one remembered having seen her the morning before. The druggist at a store at Baxter and Broadway knew her well but had not noticed her walk by the previous morning. This suggested only that she had not walked as far as the school, as the store would not have been on her way to the church. The area was, according to maps of the time, almost completely residential, with small businesses. On the route to the church, Alma would have passed a number of homes. Captain Portman waited through the night for some word from the officers searching diligently for any clue.

Speculation on the mysterious disappearance ran rampant in Louisville. Although Louisville was a highly populated city for the time, such crimes were still unusual. The newspaper reported that there seemed to be some plan afoot by whoever was holding Alma to return the child to her family, apparently based on the

EIGHT-YEAR OLD GIRL IS MISSING

F. Kellner Believes Daughter Has Been Kidnaped.

Left Home Yesterday Morning To Attend Mass.

Child Has Not Been Heard From Since.

Father Connected With Central Consumers' Company.

POLICE SCOURING THE CITY.

Headline in the *Courier-Journal*, December 10, 1909.

observation by reporters that her father appeared to be "more or less calm and collected" most of the time. The *Courier-Journal* reported that it was "practically certain" that an important development was imminent but was a "carefully guarded secret." The police force of the entire county was on alert, and "every clew in the possession of the police has been run to earth." At about 8:30 a.m., Gus Gutgsell, the keeper of a saloon at 1420 South Preston street, near the railroad crossing, called Fred Kellner to report that a customer had informed him that he had seen a child resembling Alma's description the afternoon before, "near the end of the Eighteenth-street car line." Another report was made by Gus Schadd, a barber who worked at Jackson and Madison streets, claiming he saw two women put a girl wearing a red hat trimmed with a plain ribbon into a yellow wagon. He could not recall the time, however. Yet another witness, Fred Wile, stated that he had encountered a child at Preston and Breckinridge streets who appeared lost and asked how to get to Clay and Caldwell streets.

Louisville police detectives Ross and Condley, who had been stationed at the Kellner residence all night, were pulled away Thursday morning, and the house was left unguarded until dark, when Patrolman McHugh was assigned and arrived to take a post. On Friday morning, the *Courier-Journal*, the morning newspaper, reported that the day before, a former maid of the Kellners, Katie Martin, had brought information to Mrs. Kellner concerning a meeting about Alma that she had had with a man and a man dressed as a woman. There was a rumor of a planned meeting between the two men and Mrs. Kellner with an aim to arranging for Alma's return. The maid had worked for the Kellners before Alma's birth, and the reporters were told by Captain Portman that there was to be news forthcoming at 1:30 a.m.; nothing, however, developed.

Captain Portman was quoted as saying that he did not believe that offering a reward for Alma's return would be helpful, and it was noted that Fred Kellner himself did not have the wherewithal to pay a ransom at any rate. However, it was assumed that Kellner's wealthier relatives would supply funds for Alma's return, if needed. It was noted that detectives had visited Kellner's widowed stepmother Thursday morning and that she conferred with her stepson as well. The idea that there was any attempt to gather funds by the family to pay a ransom was denied. Fred and Florence both expressed confidence that their daughter would soon be home.

Minnie Kellner, Alma's nine-year-old sister, a boarding student at the Sacred Heart Academy on "the Cherokee road," was brought home but was perhaps not told why, although certainly she knew her parents were

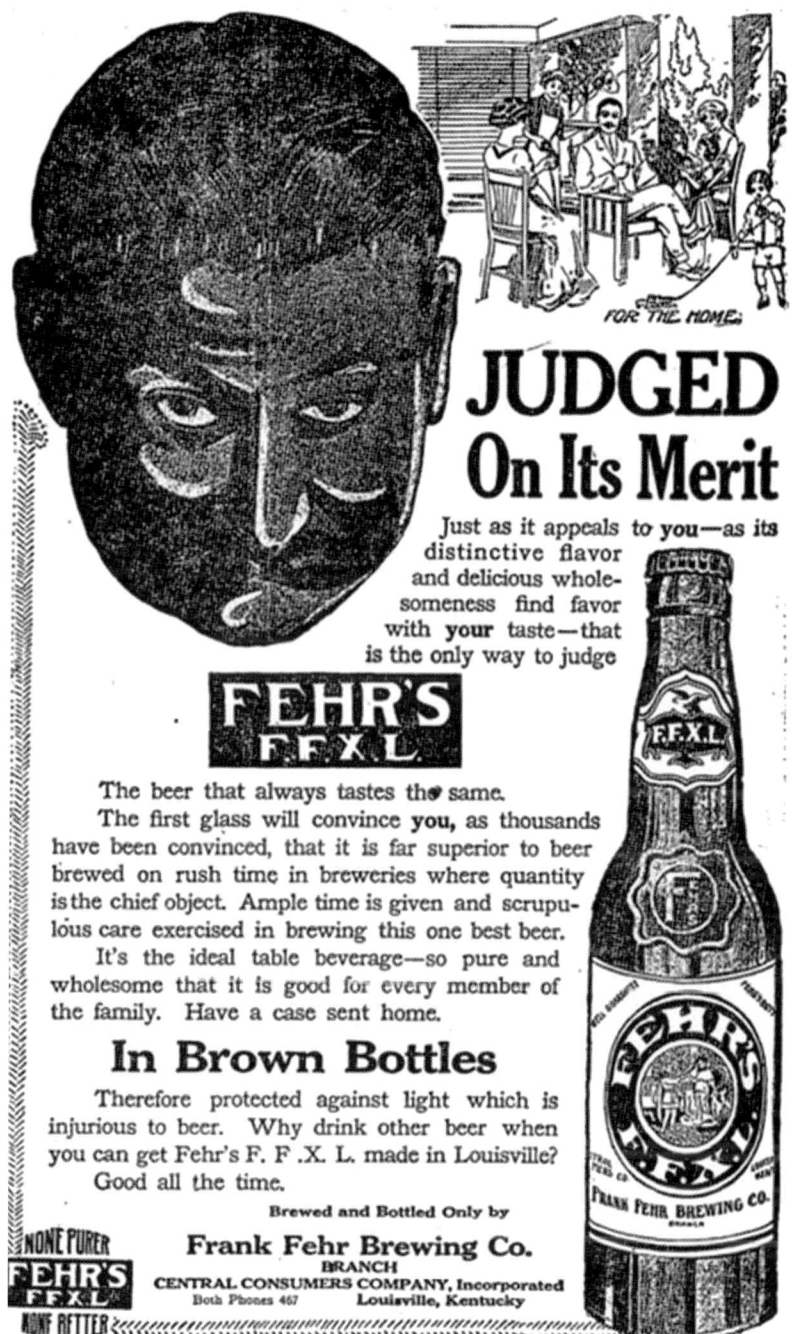

Advertisement for the Frank Fehr Brewing Company, published in the *Courier-Journal*.

distraught. She was given only a brief visit with her parents before being hurried a few blocks away to the home of her grandmother, Mrs. J.F. Kellner, at 312 East Broadway, where she could be better sheltered from the news of her little sister. (Although not mentioned, her young brother was presumably also sent to the grandmother.)

Major Patrick Ridge, the night chief, provided reporters with his own strong theory of the case. He expressed concern that he had trouble dragging facts from Mr. Kellner—facts that should have been provided voluntarily. Ridge noted that he "would never have gotten the information I needed in working up the case if I had not gotten it on the outside and presented it to him." He continued: "There are a great many things that look suspicious. We were not informed of the absence of the child until the trail had grown stale. We are watching people in two cities. So far, we have heard nothing from them. Sometimes I think that it isn't a real kidnaping case for ransom."

Officers stationed at the house were not told of the planned meeting between Mrs. Kellner and the unknown couple, but they did later observe that they had noticed the "lifting of the pall of uneasiness" over the child's absence. Mrs. Kellner told reporters that she would go after her daughter alone but refused to say whether a ransom would be paid, even avoiding the word entirely.

Newspaper reporters stationed at the home reported the family's every move, going so far as to note their bedtime. The reporters had, according to Fred, completely taken over the home. Alma's father was specifically questioned about plans to drag the nearby Beargrass Creek, only a few blocks away, but it was noted that a body would normally surface within forty-eight hours. Officers from every city within two hundred miles remained on high alert and were running down clues all day Thursday.

By Thursday, Captain John P. Carney, the Louisville chief of detectives, had taken personal charge of the case. He communicated with officers in towns and cities throughout the state, and even the country, to be on the lookout for the missing girl. He went to the Ohio River wharf to determine if any of the boats docked there had taken a child aboard. He telegraphed other ports to ask that boats that had left Louisville since Wednesday morning be searched.

Frank Fehr, the current president of the Central Consumers Company and Fred Kellner's cousin, along with several other members of the family, searched the city in Fehr's "big red touring car." Frank Fehr would soon become the official family spokesman.

Louisville's Alma Kellner Mystery

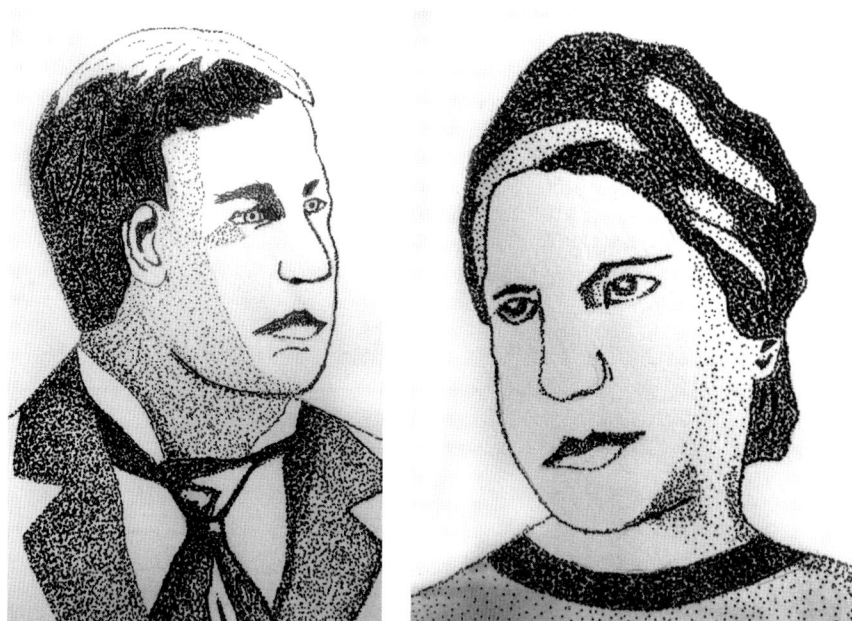

Left: Frederick Kellner. *Right*: Florence Kellner. *Original illustrations by Melanie Hilliard.*

The chief of police, H. Watson Lindsey, when questioned on Thursday night, stated that the area around the home and the church had been very closely searched, so minutely that it seemed "hardly possible" that anything had been overlooked. He assured the reporters that all the family members, friends and employees of the family, including former servants, had been questioned and had provided adequate alibis. In addition, "every police character [had] given an account of himself."

3
The Investigation

The *Courier-Journal* noted that, while there had been situations in Louisville of family abductions—a child being taken by a separated parent—there had never "been a real sensational kidnaping case" in the city. The law at the time for kidnapping, found in the Kentucky Statutes, Section 1221, read as follows:

> *Arresting, imprisoning, or transporting another—aiding and abetting—If any person or persons shall arrest or imprison another, or shall transport him, against his will, beyond the bounds of this Commonwealth, otherwise than according to law, or cause, or in any manner counsel, aid or abet in such arrest, imprisonment, or transportation, the person or persons so offending shall, on conviction thereof, be deemed guilty of felony, and shall be confined in the penitentiary not less than one nor more than twenty years.*

By the reporting on December 11, there was already concern expressed that the witnesses were giving different accounts. The former servant, Katie Martin, refuted the news account the day before and denied that she had given information to Mrs. Kellner or that she had seen Alma the day she disappeared. However, the police seemed convinced that the kidnapper had been in contact with Mrs. Kellner, despite Martin's denials. The *Courier-Journal* reported that Martin had clearly conveyed a message to Mrs. Kellner that eased her mind considerably. Martin had also specifically told several reporters that she had been met by two people, at least one of whom was a man, but both were dressed as women, who wanted to set up a meeting with Mrs. Kellner for the next morning. She claimed then that she was threatened with death if she "dared to disclose either the time or the place of the meeting" to anyone, including the police. At that time, she told the reporters that she felt sure that the meeting would prove fruitful. Unfortunately, it was believed that the meeting fell through when arrest was feared.

As is often the case in such high-profile situations, even the most minor of witnesses was visited by the diligent—and competitive—local reporters. Mr. Quillo Fontana, the owner of a saloon located at Third avenue and Green (Liberty) street, reported that on Wednesday afternoon, at about 4:00 p.m., Frederick Kellner had announced that his daughter was missing. Fontana's sister, Bessie Fontana, was Alma's godmother, which explained his knowledge. When contacted by the family, Bessie confirmed by telephone that she had not seen Alma. It seemed that although Fred was aware that Alma was not at home, as expected, he did not become apprehensive immediately. But as he talked more to his wife later in the afternoon, he realized that the situation was truly serious and began making contacts. It was also reported by Quillo that another little girl, his niece, Bessie Gatto, had been accosted by a man in a buggy some time earlier, between Jackson and Hancock streets. The man had tried to get her into his buggy. He had promised to give her a ride to school, the same school Alma attended. She escaped and ran away from him.

The offer of a substantial reward brought out a number of men who "offered their services and theories" on the case. It was reported that "all of the amateurs, after telling of their burning desires to get to work on the case, asked to be clothed with the authority of a peace officer. The police are not certain of their powers along this line. They are taking the names and addresses of the applicants and telling them that they will be informed later if their request for authority can be granted."

And, of course, psychics appeared. Freda Rinke, a "girl medium," reportedly could provide no information on Alma's disappearance. Freda, age ten, was a "medium and clairvoyant of local fame" who lived in Jeffersonville, Indiana, along with her father. She was reputed to have "mystifying powers" and had gone into trances several times at the behest of the Kellner family, but nothing had been learned. Her father and several other men from her city attended an hour-long conference with Louisville officials, including Chief Lindsey, Major Patrick Ridge and Captain Carney. Two unknown women also attended. One of the witnesses they spoke to, Ira Dorsey, stated that he'd seen a woman and a child cross the river on a ferry on the day Alma disappeared. The party of Louisville law enforcement officers was returned to the interurban ferry in vehicles owned by Mr. Fehr and the police. The exhausted officers then retired to their homes to get a little sleep.

It was reported in the newspaper on December 15 that, for the first time since the child's disappearance, Fred Kellner had, the day before, given "partial attention to his duties as general solicitor of the Central Consumers Company." Despite a request, the governor of Kentucky, Augustus E. Willson, had not yet offered a reward, given the anticipation that the child would return home. But with no additional information surfacing, it was expected that he would soon offer a reward of $500, the maximum allowed by Kentucky law from the state coffers.

By December 17, the police, having run out of clues, sent employees of the sewer and drain department to tramp through the sewers near the church with lanterns and drag the catch basins in the area near the Kellner home and the church. A "morbid throng" followed the men in their gloomy task. Unfortunately, it was noted that all the sewers in the area emptied into the Ohio River at some distance below the Waterworks, located at Zorn and River roads. Since the child's disappearance, there had been heavy rains, and it was acknowledged that the child's body may have been washed into the Ohio River. Captain Carney admitted that he had had "twenty theories, 200 clews and 1,000 tips," which had all turned out to be "bloomers"—silly mistakes. The Louisville officers continued to work everything that came to hand, and no bit of information was considered "too small or too trivial for immediate attention." It was reported that Alma's father had finally broken down from the "incessant worry and strain" and had taken to his bed, although Florence was now "bearing up in a wonderful manner."

Without a doubt, the Kellner and Fehr families endured a dismal Christmas. The year 1909 passed into 1910, and the mysterious disappearance faded from the minds of the citizens of Louisville, although certainly not from the hearts of her family and those who had known young Alma. On January 14, 1910, Joseph Wendling, the janitor of St. John's Church, took flight, abandoning his wife, Magdalena[3] Arnold Wendling, and leaving Father Schuhmann in the lurch. Neither his wife nor the priest found his disappearance to be remarkable at the time, given his past history of unreliability.

On April 15, 1910, an article on the front page of the *Courier-Journal* indicated that it was strongly suspected that Alma was "in the clutches of a gypsy band" encamped north of Los Angeles, California. It had been noted that a fair-haired, young white girl was with the "dark-skinned wanderers." The travelers had reported that they'd been through Ohio and Kentucky the year before. Deputy Sheriff Alexander was assigned to the case and expected efforts were being made to "spirit the girl away." When told this information, her uncle, Frank Fehr, admitted that he did not know if the child was Alma, but he was gratified to learn that she had not been forgotten and that the entire nation was still on the lookout for her.

4

The Discovery

On the afternoon of May 30, 1910, dramatic headlines flashed across the state. It appeared that Alma Kellner had been found, only a few hundred feet, if that, from where she had last been seen. However, the timing was such that the news in Louisville was disseminated first by telephone and word of mouth. Certainly, within only a few hours, most of the members of the community knew what had occurred.

With the *Courier-Journal* being a morning publication, and Louisville's primary newspaper, it was not until May 31 that local headlines trumpeted: "Arrest Follows Discovery of Alma Kellner's Mutilated Body." The story detailed how Richard Baxter Sweet, who lived at 433 Garden street, had been assigned by his employer, Haller and Zehnder, a plumbing company at Underhill and Broadway, to pump out water that had collected in the cellar of the old school building located on the church property. The building, no longer in use for that purpose, was situated directly to the east of the St. John's rectory. Although described in the stories as a plumber, his employer later clarified that Sweet was a laborer, assigned to do the dirty work of emptying the space of water so that the leak could be located and repaired. Sweet had started the work of pumping out the cellar on Saturday and had returned on Monday to finish the work, after the water had gone down sufficiently to allow him to find the presumed leak. At about 9:30 a.m., while in the process of locating the source of the water, he entered a subcellar that had also filled with water. As Sweet put his shovel into the "little narrow corner of the cellar just under the street," he nearly retched from a "fearful odor." In probing with his shovel, Sweet came across a roll of old carpet and spotted a tiny shoe in a pile of rubbish. He pulled at the carpet and made a horrifying discovery, as he uncovered a small skeleton.

Horrified, Sweet immediately scrambled up the ladder, passed through the trapdoor and rushed out into the late spring morning. He "unfolded his harrowing experience to a passerby" and then ran to a telephone at a nearby store to call the First District Police station, located on Shelby street, near Market street. Captain George M. Brown and Lieutenant M.J. Rawley answered the call and hastened to the scene and soon "flashed hurry calls" to police headquarters located at the central station, based in city hall. Within minutes, Chief Watson and Captain Carney dashed to the scene and started a preliminary investigation with the other officers who'd also answered the emergency summons. They then called for the Jefferson County coroner, Dr. Ellis Duncan. Deputy Coroner William Kammerer actually arrived first, with Dr. Duncan close behind.

After examining the body in situ, with the help of Sweet, Deputy Kammerer placed the pitiful remains in a basket, and the two men raised the basket to the surface. The basket was transported to the undertaker's business location, L.D. Bax, only a few blocks away, on Chestnut street near Shelby street. The body was at the undertaker's within two hours of discovery, and Coroner Duncan soon followed it. By 11:30 a.m., Duncan, assisted by Kammerer, began his work at the undertaker's office, which served as the official site for such examinations, the city lacking its own official morgue and autopsy location.

Coroner Duncan, assisted by Deputy Coroner Kammerer, had placed the skeleton, still wrapped in the carpet, on the marble slab. Flesh fell from the bones at his touch. Using a gentle stream of water, he carefully washed the mass of flesh and bone. He screened the water and collected every scrap that might prove useful in the investigation. He discovered that the right foot, as well as the top and left side of the skull, were missing, along with all the clothing but for the stocking and little shoe on the left foot. It took the two men five painstaking hours to clean the skeleton and search for some means to make a positive identification. After finishing the examination, late in the afternoon, Coroner Duncan concluded that many more bones were missing, but a full determination had to wait for a complete inventory of what was recovered. However, he concluded that the bones collected thus far showed that the victim had been "murdered in a most brutal and inhuman manner," as the bones in the right leg were broken between the knee and the ankle, all the ribs on one side were shattered and the skull appeared to have been

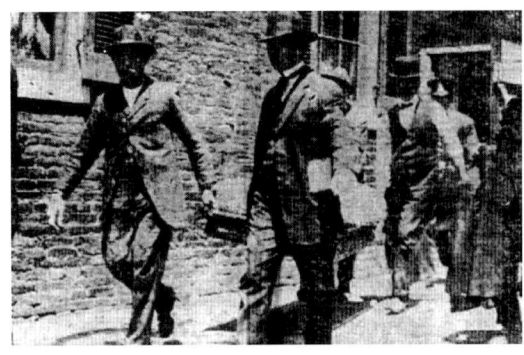

"Basket Containing All That Remains of Little Alma Kellner," published in the *Courier-Journal*.

crushed. He also discovered that some of the bones were charred, leading them to believe that the killer had tried to burn the body. This would also, it was assumed, account for the missing clothing. Coroner Duncan could not discount the possibility that quicklime may have also been used to speed the decomposition of the body.

As the autopsy progressed, Captain Carney stayed behind to examine the entire premises and oversee the excavation of the location where the body was found. A great deal of soil and debris in the subcellar was collected and removed in buckets. His search of the building yielded several clues, including more of the carpet identical to that which wrapped the body. He also collected Wendling's clothing, left behind in the room he had shared with his wife. Both the carpet and the clothing were to be examined by the city chemist, Dr. Vernon Robins, to determine if human blood was present.

Frank Fehr was immediately notified of the discovery of the body, which was, of course, presumed by all to be Alma Kellner. Although Fred Kellner was in the office, Fehr did not notify him, leaving that unenviable task to his brother-in-law George Kremer, who was secretary of the company. (Kremer was married to Frank Fehr's sister, Elizabeth.) Fehr, acting as the family representative, hurried the short distance to the church and was in time to accompany his young cousin's body to Bax's establishment. He examined the shoe that had been taken from the left foot and confirmed that it appeared to be one of Alma's shoes. He also looked at strands of hair recovered and washed by the coroner and acknowledged it was the same color as Alma's. At the same time, the Louisville police chief and the mayor, William O. Head, conferred with Reverend George Schuhmann in the rectory. Schuhmann had learned of the discovery only when he saw the police milling around the church.

Within a short time, Mrs. Lena Wendling, who had remained with the rectory after her husband's disappearance, was ordered taken to police headquarters for a "severe grilling" in Captain Carney's office. She stated that her maiden name was Arnold and that she was from Alsace, Germany.[4] She indicated that her absent husband, Joseph, was from Genlis, Côte D'or, France. She claimed that they'd married at St. Peter's Church, located in the California neighborhood at Seventeenth and Garland streets, and that she had come to Kentucky because her brother Alois Arnold already lived in Louisville.[5] Lena Wendling, who had lived at the rectory for six months, claimed that she knew nothing of the subcellar. She talked reluctantly but said that Joseph had deserted her on January 14 without explanation, the same day Frank Fehr had called on Father Schuhmann about Alma's disappearance. Neither she nor Father Schuhmann had reported him to the police as missing because, she admitted, Joseph was "noted for indifference in the performance of his duties" and had deserted employers before. She stated that he was twenty-seven and she was forty-two and that he'd been arrested previously for "fooling with girls at Bryant and

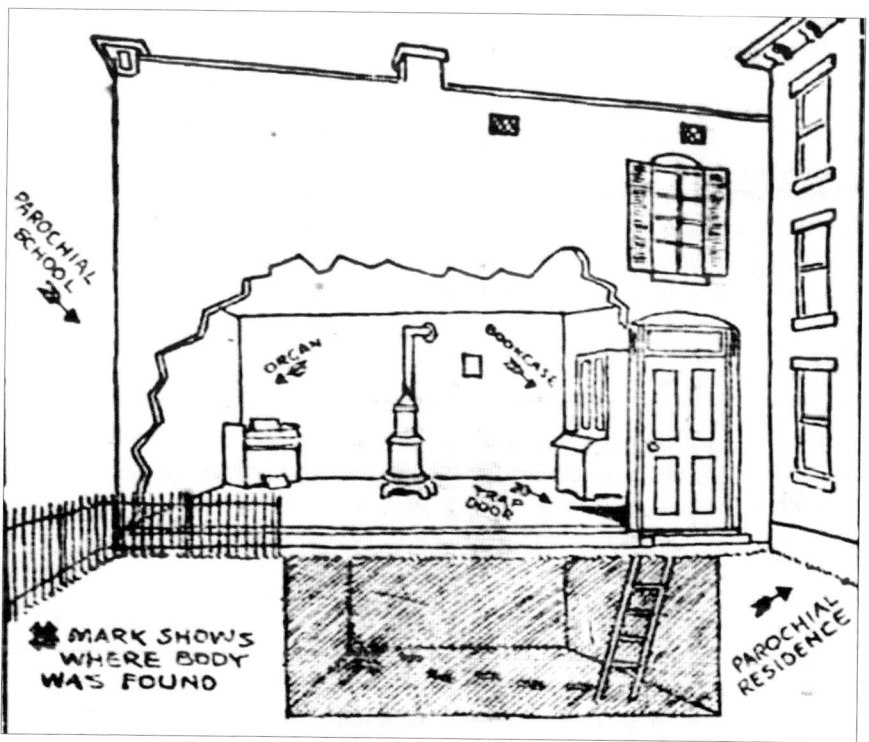

Illustration of the inside of the schoolhouse where Alma Kellner's body was found, as published in the *Courier-Journal*.

Stratton's College," a Louisville business college, for which he'd been fined in police court.

Following the questioning, Captain Carney and Detective Charles Simons returned to the St. John's rectory, where they again went to the room once shared by the Wendlings. They looked for clothing possibly worn by Joseph Wendling and found stained men's clothing. Lena Wendling claimed she had washed the clothes and had disposed of an old hat of Wendling's by tossing it into an ash barrel. Upon further searching, however, they found the hat she had claimed to have thrown away. On the brim and the crown, the officers found similar suspicious stains. They also found a small gold ring and a "little pewter skirt or waist pin," the latter of which was later identified by Florence Kellner as belonging to her daughter. Florence was doubtful about the ring, however, although Captain Carney was convinced it did belong to Alma. Lena Wendling could not offer any explanations about the origin of the items, even though they were found in the trunk in her room. She claimed that a little boy had found them and "left them with her." She wept piteously and insisted to the Jefferson County Jail matron, Mrs. Miller, that she knew nothing about the crime with which she was suspected as being an accessory. She told the matron that she was sure her husband "never knew the little girl." All of the clothing was sent on to Dr. Robins for examination and testing for blood.

Lena Wendling withdrew a statement she'd made earlier, "to the effect that she refused to advance money to her husband when he left" and that he had withdrawn $190 of her money from the bank without her consent. Father Schuhmann, when asked by newspaper reporters about his former janitor, stated that he preferred to remain silent until something had been made definite about the crime, in fairness to those who might be suspects. He admitted that he had hired the Wendlings on November 9, 1909, as janitor and housemaid, respectively. He further stated that the keys to the school building under which the child's body was found were always available to Joseph Wendling, as they were usually left hanging on a doornail in the kitchen.

He recalled nothing suspicious from the day Alma disappeared, only stating that he had last seen Wendling around noon that day, when dinner was served.

On the night the child disappeared, Father Schuhmann continued to the newspaper reporters, the room above which the skeleton was found was used by members of the Young Ladies' Sodality, a social organization. They had met there that day for the purpose of taking on new members. The building had not been used for school purposes for years and was located to the east of the rectory. The walls of the two buildings were separated only by the width of a passageway. This convinced the police that the child was not murdered in that room, as they presumed some evidence would have been discovered by the young women. A report being circulated that Detective Steve Condley had inspected the subcellar was denied by that officer, who stated that he had been totally unaware of the existence of the space, accessed through a trapdoor in the floor.

Father Schuhmann stated he, too, had been unaware of the cellar until the week before, when Benedict Thomas, the new janitor, reported that the cellar had become filled with water. Thomas, hearing the splash of dripping water and investigating the source of the sound, had only then discovered the space. He prompted Father Schuhmann to engage the plumbing service to drain the water and repair the presumed leaking pipe. The priest reported that Sweet and Jacob Haller had worked all day on Saturday to drain the water, getting it down to about a foot before they left for the day. During that time, Haller had waded around in the location where the body was later found. On Monday morning, Sweet and a helper returned and set the pump to work again, at the same time digging a ditch to allow a way for the remaining water to seep out of the cellar.

When notified that the child's body had been found on the premises, Father Schuhmann immediately dismissed the pupils of the school. The children departed, many crying. Certainly some of the children of the small school would have known Alma Kellner. As the news quickly spread in the neighborhood, it was estimated that hundreds of people "came running from every direction"; order was maintained only with the greatest difficulty. Police were stationed around the church and school, and spectators were kept on the opposite sides of Walnut and Clay streets, away from the church.

Chief Lindsey offered his opinion that the child had been "accosted and taken to her death while kneeling in prayer" at the church. It was reported by Sister Genevieve, the sister superior at the Academy of Our Lady of Mercy, the child's school, that Alma Kellner was very devout and was often found kneeling in prayer in the school's chapel, alone.

St. John's Church was, of course, once again searched thoroughly. The first discovery of interest was made by Deputy Coroner Kammerer, who had returned to the scene after assisting Dr. Duncan with the autopsy. While searching the inside of the sanctuary, he was on the lookout for marks on the walls and floors when he spotted a little closet near the entrance, just under the east belfry. When he opened the door of the small space, he found a woman's sleeveless ribbed undershirt, rolled into a ball and tucked into a corner. It exhibited great spots of red, apparently blood, around one of the armholes and in the parts that covered the chest and the back. It was collected for examination by the city chemist.

Since the only place for the child's body to have been burned in the immediate vicinity of where it was found was in one of the cellar furnaces below the church, it was believed that it was taken there initially. Then, for some reason, the killer abandoned the attempt to burn her body. Access to the furnaces was usually down stairs that led from an outside door on the east side of the church and into the cellar, but it was also possible to get down into the area through a trapdoor in the church sacristy, on the west side of the building, closest to Clay street. From there, if a person dropped down through that trapdoor, they would be on a narrow ledge composed of the clay that also served as the walls and floor of the cellar, an area that had apparently not yet been truly explored.

Richard Hite, an employee of the city, entered the cellar under the church the next morning to more closely examine the space. At about 10:50 a.m., while rummaging through the ash pile on the embankment, near a flue in the wall, he "threw a pile of clinkers [the stony residue from burned coal or from a furnace] aside and the little foot rolled from the ledge and fell into the passageway." He did not initially realize what had fallen, but he finally climbed down to investigate what he'd tossed. In the dim light, he still could not be sure what the item was, so he carried it up to the outside and showed it to George S. Dusenberry, a foreman in the street cleaning department who was overseeing the process. When Dusenberry spotted two tiny toes "protruding from the charred mass," he called for Deputy Coroner Kammerer, who was nearby. Kammerer, in turn, called for Frank Fehr and Coroner Duncan, still inside the church. Duncan, recognizing that what was found was a human foot, "commissioned his deputy to take charge of the ragged little member until he could hold an examination." The small foot was still partially enclosed by the remains of a leather shoe.

After a further search, just under that trapdoor from the sacristy, a lady's handkerchief, a glove, a feather, a crucifix and a pearl bead were found on the ledge. With the tiny foot discovered to have been left behind in the church cellar, Chief Lindsey came to the opinion that the body was hacked up there, in the cellar. He believed that the killer initially thought of burning the corpse limb by limb, since several limbs were missing, but that at some point that plan was abandoned. From that point, presumably, the body could have been removed via the cellar steps, around the back of the parish

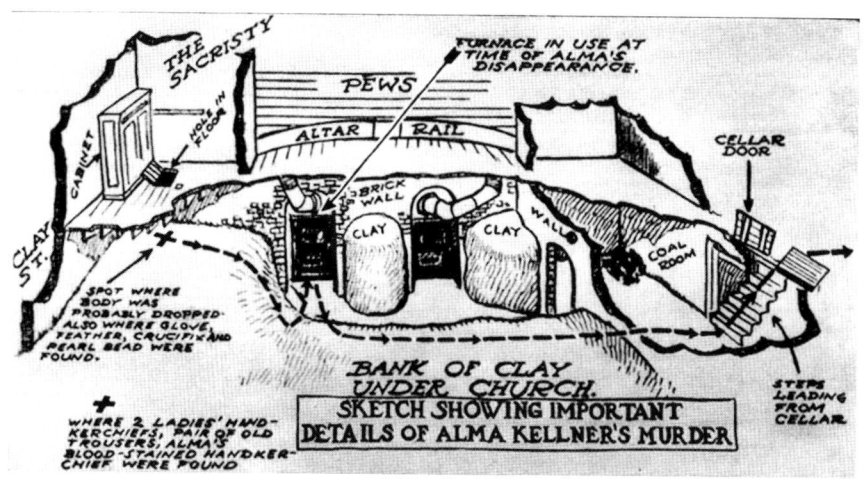

Sketch of the basement area of St. John's Church, as published in *True Detective Mysteries*.

residence and then into the school building. At the time, the side wall of the parochial school was directly connected to the rear wall of the church. A brick wall completed the enclosure to the east, preventing any passersby from seeing anything that might go on inside the courtyard. It was noted that the killer had to be very familiar with the location where the body was found, since "this was the one place in a thousand to conceal the body of a victim, and a thousand detectives might have gone there a hundred times without ever suspecting that the secret of the mystery was so near to them." Even the parish priest did not know the hole, the subcellar, was there, and it was only after it was cleared that it was found to be more than a few feet deep. Presumably, the existence of the cellar itself was known by some, as the trapdoor was clearly visible in the floor of a room in regular use, but it went unused. And the actual location where the body was found was a form of a subcellar later described by elderly congregants as an old cistern, present before the school building was constructed over it. It was noted that the body was found in a scooped-out location, indicating that the place had been prepared in some way to receive the corpse.

All of the ashes and clinkers that had been thrown in on top of the ledge in the furnace room were hauled up the steps and out into the alley. The detritus was thoroughly sifted, using a cart covered with a screen. All of the items of importance had been collected by 1:15 p.m. Before leaving, however, Deputy Coroner Kammerer, in an attempt to be thorough, crawled inside both furnaces and squeezed up inside the large round pipes that connected

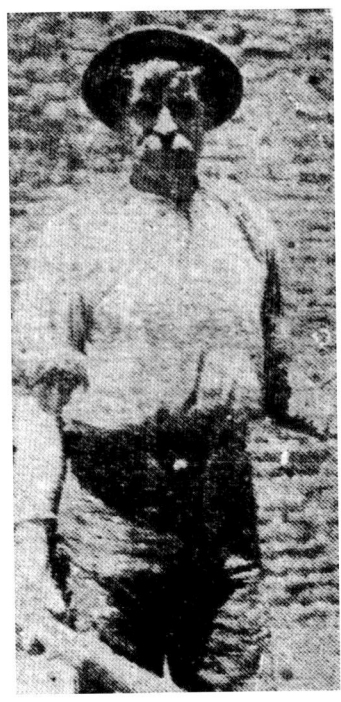

"Richard Baxter Sweet, Plumber, Who Discovered the Little Girl's Body—View of the Cellar Door," published in the *Courier-Journal*.

with the ventilators near the altar, but he found nothing more of interest. The ashes were hauled to the city stables, near Eighth and Zane streets, to be sifted once again. The little foot was taken by the coroner, to be cleaned and studied; the undershirt was dispatched to Dr. Robins, the city chemist, to determine if the spots were blood.

Once the coroner completed his exam, Frank Fehr, speaking for the family, made a statement: "I entertained the theory all along that the child had met with foul play, but in desperation I clung to the kidnaping theory in order to buoy up the hopes of the family. When no one came forward and offered to negotiate with us to return the child for a ransom I felt sure that she would not be found alive, but nevertheless I hoped that our worst fears would not be realized."

Fehr indicated that he had received, early on, positive information that young Alma had managed to reach the church that morning, by the testimony of a woman who had been at the church. However, the woman had not paid the child any special attention and could not say how she had left the church. The family was asked about a gold ring the child had been known to wear, but none had been found in the subcellar. Although the child had several fillings in her jaw teeth, only three jaw teeth had been found at that point, and none were filled.

With the body found and a homicide confirmed, the investigation moved forward. There seemed little doubt that Alma had been seized at the church, possibly while kneeling in prayer at the altar. Sister Mary Genevieve extolled the devotion shown by the little girl, who would often slip away for a few moments of prayer at school. The chief agreed that while he could not be sure of what had happened, of course, the theory that she was taken while praying at the altar was the most plausible one available at the time. Chief Lindsay detailed to the waiting newspaper reporters that he believed Alma was seized and taken to the basement of the church, as that was the only location where the body could have been burned. He expressed his belief that the child's body had been hacked up in preparation for burning but that something had happened to prevent it, and that explained the missing pieces of the body. Instead, he suggested, the killer resorted to quicklime to complete his gruesome task. George Kremer brought an old shoe of the child to the undertaker, who compared it to the one found with the child and found it to be the exact counterpart, presumably the same size. This was considered to leave no question as to the identification of the body as that of Alma Kellner. It was also noted that other facts confirmed the identification, including that the body was near the scene of her disappearance, that it had been "decaying for months" and that no other child had been reported missing.

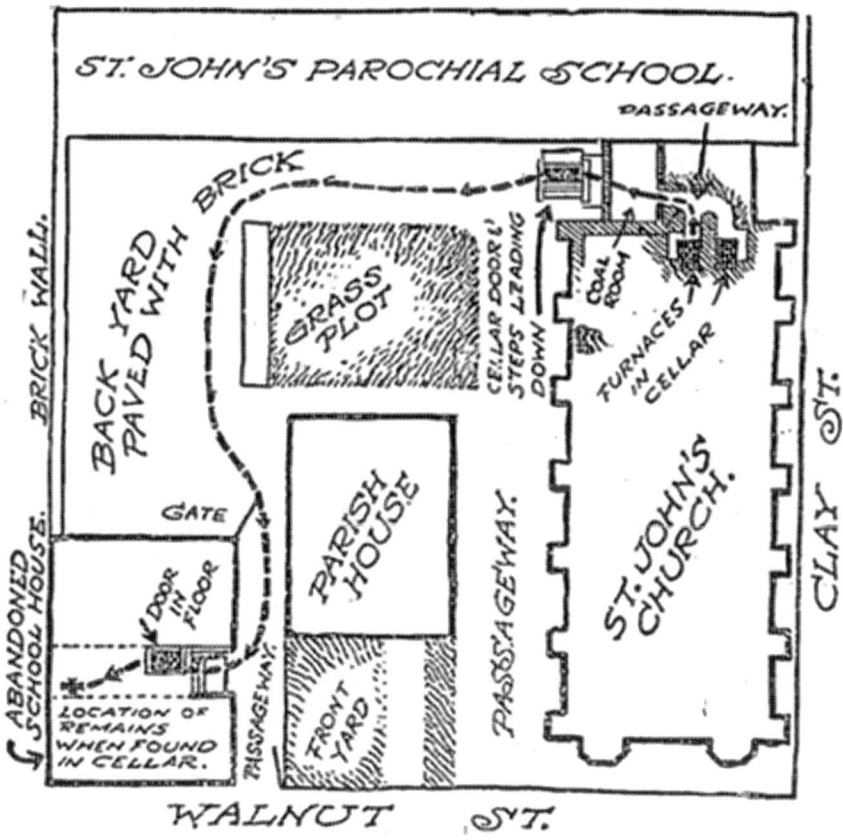

"Diagram Showing Location of the Church, Parish House and School." The arrows in the drawing indicate the course that the murderer of Alma Kellner may have taken if he attempted to burn her body before burying it in the cellar under the schoolhouse, published in the *Courier-Journal*.

Given the secluded nature of the hiding place, the chief agreed that the killer had to be intimately familiar with the premises, given the general lack of knowledge about the cellar. He presumed that the body had been moved at night to the location where it was found, since no one had witnessed it in the small space on the day of the disappearance.

The *Louisville Times* gave a detailed description of the gruesome condition of the body, as reported by the coroner.

> *Head, split open from the forehead back to the base of the brain, as though it had been done with some heavy instrument. On the right side of the head the cut was clean. On the left side it extended down to the jaw bone.*
>
> *The right shoulder blade is intact. The right arm is attached to it as far as the elbow. The right hand is missing. The left arm and shoulder blade were found detached, but nearby the body.*
>
> *The left [sic] to the ankle was found on the right side. The leg and foot of the right side was broken, but still attached to the torso.*
>
> *Practically all of the flesh is gone. The heart and the vital organs are intact and in their proper positions. The bones are all broken and the ends are seared.*
>
> *The body was nude with the exception of the pair of shoes.*

The "broken, searched and denuded skeleton, with the little shoes and the few locks of hair," was placed in a casket in preparation for burial.

The day after the discovery of the body, Frank Fehr offered a $1,000 reward for the arrest and conviction of his young cousin's killer. (This mirrored a reward he had offered earlier for the return of the child.)

Detective Pat White carried the clothing found in the Wendlings' room, a blue flannel shirt and black trousers, to Dr. Vernon Robbins, the city chemist and bacteriologist, for an analysis of the stains. Detective Charles Hickey was assigned to oversee the "sewer gang" that was excavating "all the ooze and mud" from the cellar under the school, at the direction of the coroner. All of the "grewsome mass" was to be removed in wagons to the morgue, to be washed free of the mud, in the hope that the missing "parts of Alma Kellner" would be found.

Despite Mrs. Kellner's uncertainty about whether the ring and the pin found in the Wendlings' belongings were her daughter's, the family accepted that the body was that of their missing child. It was noted that Joseph Wendling was now the primary suspect and "being searched for by the police departments of the civilized world." The distraught Mrs. Kellner, however, expressed confusion as to why her daughter's body was not brought home "or how there should be any doubt about the identification." The newspaper reported that she mentioned that the child could easily be identified by a scar on her nose, as a result of a fall from her roller skates.

Chief Carney charged that Lena Wendling was hiding information, as she had made several conflicting statements. For example, she claimed that she had no photo of her husband, yet one was found in her meager possessions. Benedict Thomas, the janitor who had taken Joseph Wendling's place, stated that he had seen Wendling one day in February pass by the school and gaze up into the windows. If true, that indicated that Wendling had not left town immediately upon his disappearance but had returned to the church, perhaps looking for his wife.

Captain Carney stated that "Mrs. Wendling is a woman of a low order of intelligence, and it is with the greatest of difficulty that we are able to get anything out of her." She kept repeating to the officers that Joseph had been "good to her, kind to her."

The officers had been told that Joseph Wendling had been arrested the year before on a charge of being in the company of a female student in one of the business colleges, and they were dutifully searching the police court for an official copy of the record, if any existed. However, a detailed search of police and other legal records revealed no evidence of actual charges placed against him at that time.

As information spread about the search for Wendling, Mayor Head's secretary, Charles Foster, reported that about two months previously, a Frenchman had asked for "pauper transportation" to Montreal, Canada. He'd claimed an occupation of a janitor, but Foster was positive it was not Wendling. The stenographer in the office, E.L Eilson, agreed. It was noted that Wendling apparently had "plenty of funds" when he departed.

The carpet in which the body had been rolled had dried and was closely examined. It did not match any of the pieces of carpet found around the church and the school.

School had been cancelled at St. John's following the discovery of the body and was expected to be closed for several more days. Father Schuhmann was very distressed by the situation and remained at home, receiving hundreds of sympathy messages. He saw only close friends and insistent members of the press. He engaged two private detectives, former captains in the police department, James Kinnarney and J.T. Larkin, to assist in the investigation. Larkin stayed with the priest at the rectory, presumably to ward off visitors. As part of the investigation, officers had seized a bundle of correspondence in French from the Wendlings' belongings and were having them translated.

On May 31, 1910, at the Bax undertaking establishment, the small skeleton of Alma Kellner, without the small foot later found in the church, was placed in a small, white casket. The casket bore a silver plate on the lid with the inscription "Our Darling." Henry Bosse conducted the brief service at the undertaker's. A white hearse, accompanied by a single carriage with the mourners, carried the casket to its final resting place in St. Louis Cemetery, on Baxter avenue. The burial was a quiet, simple affair, with only three men in attendance: George Kremer, Andrew Fehr and John Schwartz. (Frank Fehr was reported to have been present, but he simply saw them off at the undertaker and did not accompany the group to the cemetery.) No religious services were held at the time, although it was believed that when her parents could do so, a funeral Mass would be held later. Alma's "heartbroken parents had not sufficiently recovered from the dreadful shock to be present" as their daughter was finally laid to rest.

5
THE PRELIMINARIES

With the child finally buried, the focus turned to the investigation. For the next several days, the Louisville police concentrated on the legal preliminaries necessary to make a case against any eventual suspect.

On June 2, Coroner Duncan and Captain Carney met in the latter's office to discuss what had been done and what still needed to be done. The coroner had not yet scheduled an inquest, but it would be the "natural preliminary" to any further investigation, as well as being a legal requirement. But in such a situation, it was acknowledged, there was much work to be done before the inquest could even be contemplated.

The rewards offered for the arrest of the murderer continued to accumulate. The City of Louisville, through its lower body, the Louisville General Council, authorized $2,500, which, added to the amount already pledged, raised the potential reward to $6,000. The goal was to reach $10,000. In addition to the large pledges, various citizens were offering small amounts. These interlocking rewards would later prove a conundrum for those who offered them.

As usual in such high-profile cases, witnesses with even the smallest tidbit of information of possible interest began to come forward. Peter Herbst, a driver for a Neider's grocery on the northwest corner of Shelby street and Broadway, identified Mrs. Wendling as the person who had accepted a basket of lime, along with a half barrel of sand, from him at the church sometime prior to the previous Christmas but after Alma had gone missing. He had delivered it via the passageway into the brickyard behind the priest's residence and placed it in a shed there. He was given the opportunity to identify Mrs. Wendling in an informal lineup of several women at the jail and immediately picked her out as the person who had accepted the lime. She was questioned by private detective Kinnarney, who was assisting the police in the case, but she denied having ever received lime from any source. Reverend Schuhmann denied knowing anything about an order of lime during that time, although he acknowledged that it had been used previously, when Thomas was the janitor, to repair the blackboards in the school. It could not be confirmed by the coroner at that time whether lime had actually been used on the child's body to hasten the decomposition.

Another witness, Ralph Wolff, reportedly had seen Joseph Wendling on the street some days before, but upon further inquiry it was soon determined that he had made a mistake and instead had seen Benedict Thomas, the current janitor.

Lena Wendling, in the meantime, was still in jail, accused of being an accessory to the murder. Attorney Delos B. Rogers, representing her, made a motion to Judge Samuel Boldrick that charges against her be dismissed and that she be released. He raised the issue that Section 1129 of the Kentucky Statutes did not allow for a charge of accessory after the fact simply because the individual was the wife of a principal in a crime. The judge agreed to review the matter but suggested that Rogers work toward getting her released on bail. Lena was being kept in solitary confinement, with no visitors, and had been moved from the "first offenders' ward" to cells in the rear of the women's section of the jail, where she could be closely supervised by the matron, Mrs. Miller. Lena reportedly spent her time "gazing through the heavy iron doors and saying that she is innocent of any wrongdoing."

It was noted by the diligent newspapermen searching for stories to report that if it was established that Alma Kellner was murdered in the church, the doors of the church would have to be closed and no Mass said there until the church could be re-consecrated. This was pursuant to Catholic canon law, a reporter continued, which required that if a church had been "so desecrated by an act of violence or the shedding of human blood," it "must be blessed over by the bishop of the dioceses before the sacrifice of the mass can be celebrated within its bounds again." The newspaper reported that this rule was "laid down in what is known in ecclesiastical circles as 'The Rubrics,' or laws of the church." It was believed that if this process was, in fact, invoked, it would be the first instance known to have occurred in Louisville. When asked about it, Reverend Schuhmann refused to comment, noting only that it would be left to the Right Reverend Denis O'Donaghue, the bishop, to decide. When approached, however, Bishop O'Donaghue stated that he could not respond at the time, that it was a matter for the church alone and he would not air it "merely to satisfy the curious." The reporter went on to explain, for the edification of the paper's many Protestant readers, that the moment when the priest pronounces the words of consecration during the Mass, the "bread actually becomes the mystical body of Christ, and the wine His sacred blood." Since the tiny wafers are kept at the church, of course, a "church stained by violence cannot be a fitting resting place for the body of the Prince of Peace." In such instances, the bishop must perform the service that will "reconcile" the church to worship and is, purportedly, "one of the most lengthy known in the church." The exact rites for the ceremony that "must be used are set down in a book called the 'Pontifical,' and, according to the doctrine of the church, have such efficacy that the stains of blood are washed away and the church is again made a 'holy of holies,' where the Lord may be worshipped and His blessing implored."

With the formalities of a funeral in the past, all thoughts turned to the obvious—and only—suspect, the missing Joseph Wendling. Although Lena Wendling indicated that her husband had no relatives in the United States, police had reason to believe that he had family in New Orleans. A search was to be done there. The Jefferson County judge, Muir Weissinger, sent a letter to Governor Willson requesting that he offer the maximum award, $500, allowed under Kentucky law. The letter was required in order for the governor to do so, but the county judge had been assured that the letter was simply a formality.

The letter read as follows:

Louisville, KY., June 1, 1910.—Hon. Augustus E. Willson, Governor of Kentucky. Frankfort, Ky.

Dear Governor:

This whole community is shocked and upset by the brutal murder of little Alma Kellner, and I feel that every effort possible should be made for the capture of her murderer.

Section 1932 of the Kentucky Statutes provides that in aggravated cases of murder when the accused shall flee from justice, the Governor on petition of the Circuit or County Judge of the county may issue his proclamation offering a reward not exceeding $500 for the apprehension of the accused. Certainly this is an aggravated case of murder, and the accused has fled

French nationality, about 5 feet 10 inches tall, weighed about 150 pounds and had dark hair and mustache." She told Detective Simons that the man had acted strangely and appeared nervous when strangers called. She also stated that her guest slept but little and paced the floor at night. Every police official in the state was asked to be on the lookout, and hundreds of circulars about Wendling were mailed to law enforcement agencies. The circular described Wendling as follows:

Age 27; five feet ten or eleven inches; weight about 140 pounds; blue eyes, rather squinting; full protruding nose; heavy black eyebrows; black hair; black moustache, inclined to curl; narrow stooped shoulders; swarthy complexion; rosy cheeks. Is a Frenchman, sometimes taken for Hungarian or Italian; speaks with decided French accent; usually stands very erect with one foot extended as indicated in photograph; walks with long stride; blue tattoo on one forearm; has gun shot wound in left hand (not positive about this being left hand).

The circular went on to state:

Wendling left here about January 14, 1910, wearing a light checkered coat; cheap clothes; pointed shoes; light Alpine hat, and wore cheap pin—flue design with mother-of-pearls, on lapel of coat. Our information is that he was born in Genlis, Cote d'Or, France, and that he is a deserter from the French army. After deserting the French army he went to Alsace, Germany, where he worked on the farm of one Arnold. He left Alsace with one Madelene Arnold, and married her in this city. Since he has been in this country he has worked as a common laborer; is a drinking man and fond of women. Wendling is probably a degenerate, and has been arrested for fondling young girls.

The photograph circulated showed Joseph Wendling in a French military uniform, presumably the photo that was found in Lena Wendling's possession at the rectory.

Those with information were asked to wire the information to Chief Lindsey or Captain Carney. Lindsey also telegraphed Jacob McGavock Dickinson, the secretary of war and a friend, asking that the information be shared with army posts, should Wendling seek to take refuge there. The chief acknowledged that this was an unlikely possibility, but he did not want to fail to take any action that might "lead to results."

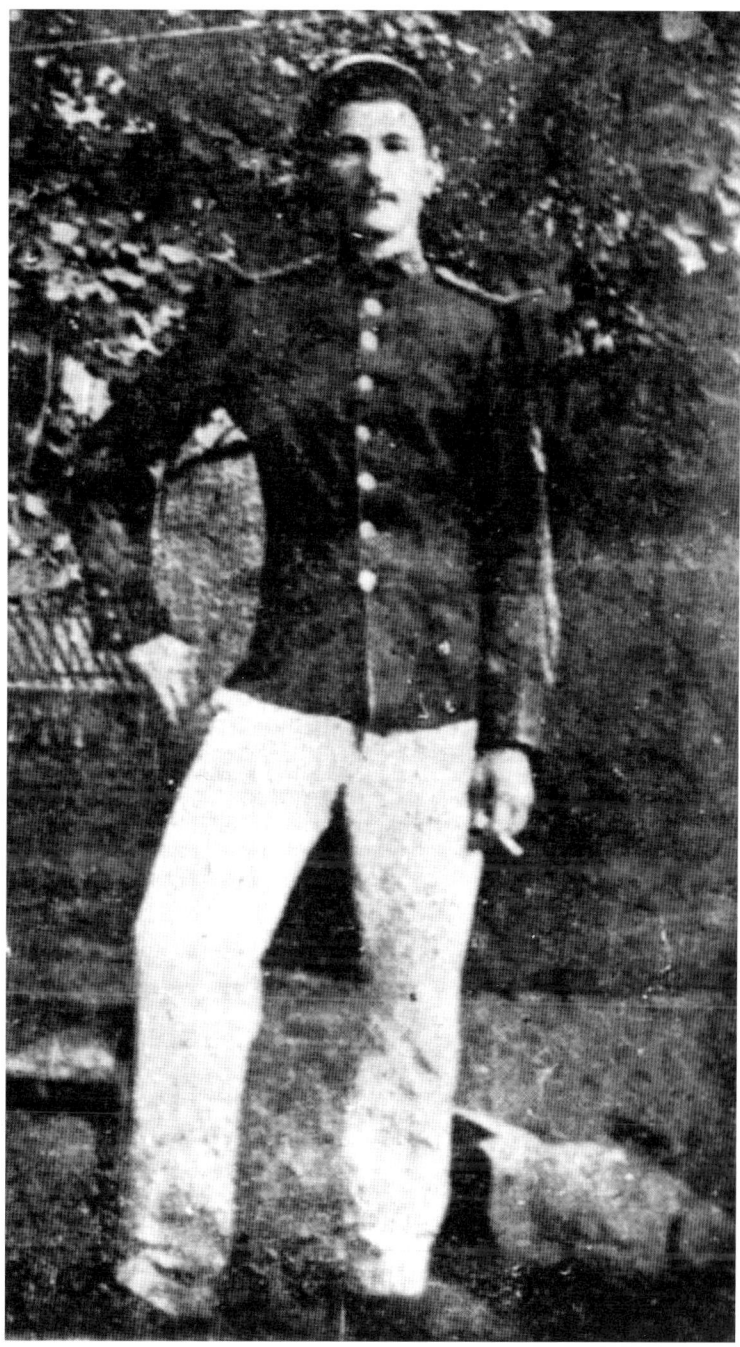

Photo of Joseph Wendling in a French military uniform. The photo was located in his belongings and used during the manhunt.

A witness came forward who supported Mrs. Wendling's claim that she did not know the whereabouts of her husband. Charles Woldich, a clerk in the local office of a steamship line, identified her as the individual who had asked him in February about whether Joseph Wendling had bought passage to Europe. When he was presented with her for identification, they clearly recognized each other and carried on a conversation in German. He stated that he had found no record of Joseph Wendling having bought a ticket from his company and had referred her to other steamship agents in town. Other agents in town, however, did not recall any similar inquiries. Her attorney made a third, vain attempt to have his client released, noting that she was unable to give bond, but Judge Boldrick concluded she should stay in jail at least until her case was called on June 8. That would give the police time to further investigate the case. On that date, he stated, he would decide if she should remain in jail or be released.

No bit of information about the case was too small for the local newspapermen. Clara Richardson, the assistant matron of the Jefferson County Jail, located at Sixth and Green (now Liberty) streets, reported that Mrs. Wendling was becoming resigned to her incarceration. Because of the strict confinement in which she was being held, she spoke little to anyone and whiled away her time in her cell, pacing and occasionally reading. She was reportedly held in a large cell, located on the south side of a long corridor, with three windows that looked out into the court below. The cell boasted three chairs, a table and two beds. The other bed was occupied by Sarah Hall, who was jailed on a minor offense. The newspaper, in painstaking detail that suggested the reporters were being paid by the word, described how Lena Wendling's bed was located in the northwest corner of the room, opening out onto the corner of the hallway. The cell had most recently been occupied by Florence Babcock, who had been just been acquitted of murdering her husband. Although Mrs. Wendling had been highly distressed immediately following her arrest, and not eating, she had settled down and was reportedly enjoying her meals. She had not asked for any writing materials, nor had she sent any letters, and no relatives had appeared. (Her brother Alois, however, later stated that he had tried to visit his sister several times and been turned away.) Lena Wendling slept well and was careful every morning to straighten her bed and make her toilet in the little bathroom located in the cell. She supposedly appeared indifferent to any publicity about her case. Since the jail lights were extinguished at 8 p.m., Mrs. Wendling usually retired by 9:00 p.m. and arose at 6:00 a.m., although inmates were not required to get out of bed until 7:00 a.m.

By June 2, although the city chemist had not yet made his formal report, it was understood that the handkerchiefs and the undershirt both bore stains that were human blood. Dr. Robins had postponed a planned vacation and was doing all the work personally, taking great care and time with his tests. Coroner Duncan was continuing his investigation as well and. for the first time, officially "ventured the opinion" that quicklime might have been used on the child's body, as he'd found a "peculiar white substance in the eye-sockets of the skeleton which has the appearance of lime." The charred foot, which had been retained by the coroner and not buried with the rest of the child's body, had been sent to the city chemist. More evidence had been found in the ashes that had been painstakingly examined at the city stables. A piece of carpet matching the pattern wrapped around the skeleton, a bit of bone believed to be part of a human rib and a small round bone believed to be one of the missing kneecaps were uncovered in the ashes being painstakingly screened.

In addition, the investigators learned that on May 2, 1910, Philip Wirth Jr. of P. Wirth & Sons, a carpentry firm, had found a shovel wedged under the floor, between two joists, of the abandoned schoolroom. Wirth had delivered a small cabinet to Father Schuhmann that day, and the priest, having just been informed by Wendling's replacement of the water in the cellar, asked the carpenter to assess the situation. Wirth had peered down into the dark void; since there were no steps, he chose not to attempt to go down, instead dropping a brick to try to determine the depth of the water. He spotted the shovel and pulled it out, giving it to Thomas, who placed it in the shed. It had been forgotten until it was mentioned by Thomas, who fetched it out to satisfy the curiosity of reporters. While there were peculiar spots on the handle (Coroner Duncan later pronounced them to be nothing more than paint, rather than blood), it was concluded that its hiding place suggested that it was likely used to dig the child's shallow grave.

The investigation marched on. By Friday, June 3, the search at the church was practically completed, with every inch of the premises having been gone over carefully. The "whole world" had been alerted as to the search for Wendling, with Scotland Yard, the Paris Prefect of Police and the Commissioner of the London Police on the mailing list for the circulars, as well as the "burgomasters of hundreds of little German villages." Assistance was offered from the outside in the person of William J. Burns, the head of the Burns-Sheridan National Detective Agency, who was passing through Louisville. Being in the business and having a natural interest, he was taken as a guest on a brief tour of the scene in the company of Chief Lindsey,

Captain Carney and others. He denied having any connection to the case and assured reporters, when asked, that he was convinced that the police were doing a proper job, despite Wendling's trail being cold by the time the child's body was found. Private detectives Kinnarney and Larkins, for the first time publicly identified as having been hired by Father Schuhmann to "run the murderer to earth," were also working hard on the case. (Today, the idea of civilians working so closely with the police to investigate a major crime seems unusual, but in the 1800s and early 1900s, only the largest police agencies had a dedicated detective force. Private detectives of various agencies, including the well-known Pinkerton Detective Agency, were very active in criminal investigations. It was common for police officers to leave public law enforcement and take positions as private investigators, either on their own or working for one of a number of well-known agencies.)

The police were kept busy running down wild rumors, with reports of Wendling having been seen near the Bernheim's distillery, on Seventeenth-street road, but no one was located. Another sighting involved a man by the name of Bigler, who bore such a striking resemblance to the missing janitor that children at St. John's School who knew Wendling, thought it was him. Bigler was apprehended but released when Father Schuhmann declared he was not Wendling. The search continued to Henderson, Kentucky, west of Louisville, where it was believed that Wendling had worked for some time in the spring. In Leeville, Louisiana, one James T. Brown, a sleight-of-hand performer (magician), was arrested, also believed to be Wendling. Another man was arrested for criminal assault in Covington, Tennessee, when he was thought to be Wendling. A report from Lexington, Kentucky, indicated that Wendling was seen on the Winchester pike, about eight miles from Lexington, and that, when spotted, he had made a "hasty departure into the woods." A report from Muncie, Indiana, came in that a man who stopped in at the home of Louis Drossman met the description of the wanted fugitive and had claimed to be sick and in need of a hospital.

It was noted on June 4 that the day before had been set as the day that Mrs. Wendling was to be placed in the "sweat box" by the police. She had remained "as stolid as ever" in her denial of any knowledge as to Joseph Wendling's whereabouts.[7]

By June 5, new theories were being advanced concerning the murder. It was believed that the crime might have been better planned than first thought when it was noted that officers had thoroughly searched the furnace room when the child was first reported missing. In fact, Sergeant Jerry Quill personally searched the basement and was escorted there by Joseph Wendling himself. He had gone back several days later and spoken to Wendling at length and later noted that if he was the guilty man, "he was the coolest criminal I have ever met." This revived the story of the visit of a mysterious woman to the grandmother's home, with the thought that the child may have initially been kidnapped and then murdered, when it was believed the child's abductors might not be able to come to terms with the family. Chief Lindsey, however, put little credence in that belief, suggesting instead that the degenerate who committed the crime may have held her body for a period of time before chopping it up and trying to burn it, and then removing it to the final grave. It was admitted that there had been no follow-up on the mysterious veiled woman who was seen and allegedly spoken to by Miss Anna Kellner, but the latter was out of town, visiting friends in Minnesota, and so could not be questioned. A mysterious and undescribed phone call to Mr. Kellner at the brewery that same day was also found to be curious and without explanation.

The police began to focus on associates of Wendling but learned he had few "intimate friends," preferring to spend most of his idle time at the picture show. One person who did know him, at least to some degree, was John Kippes, the father of Alois Arnold's deceased wife, Annie. (Annie Kippes Arnold died in 1902 and is buried in St. Louis Cemetery, along with her young daughter, who died at the age of five the year after her mother.) Kippes had known Wendling several years before, most likely since he and Magdalena Arnold had arrived in Louisville, but Kippes reportedly had not seen him in over two years. At the time, the two men had worked together at the Smith & Nixon Company.

The usual assortment of not-so-reliable tips continued to flow in. Mary Daly reported that a man meeting the description of Wendling came to her house in Louisville the Tuesday before and begged for something to eat. When she provided food, he ate ravenously and refused to speak about the murder. Her brother-in-law Gus Juliet came in with papers containing Wendling's photo, and the stranger then quickly left. It was also thought that Wendling might be hiding in the Isthmus of Panama, the Canal Zone, and a request was sent to the government there to commence a search for him. The chief had received tips that, around March 1, a man who appeared to be Wendling left New Orleans on a fruit steamer, bound for that place.

The coroner's inquest was set for June 6 but was subsequently postponed.

The succession of mistaken-identity arrests continued. A man was arrested late on Saturday, June 4, in Bowling Green, Kentucky, and was then brought to Louisville. The man, claiming to be one Jack Smith, had been found lying in a drunken stupor in Bowling Green, having become "beastly drunk" at a local soft drink stand. (At the time, soft drinks often had measurable amounts of alcohol.) The man met the description circulated for Wendling, and although he lacked a mustache, it was obvious that he had worn one previously. He also spoke with a decided French accent. Despite being interrogated ("sweated"), the man denied having done anything wrong. A local man who had just returned from Horse Cave, Kentucky, indicated that the man had been employed as a cook in a hotel there. (Although the connection was never made by the newspapermen, it is certainly possibly that this was the same individual who had been identified as having taken a room in Horse Cave.)

Initially, the two private detectives, along with Mr. Bax, the undertaker, boarded the Louisville & Nashville train for Bowling Green, having confirmed that Chief Lindsey had not, at that point, asked that the subject be brought to Louisville. Unfortunately, Squire R.S. Hunster had been ordered by Mayor Head to start with the prisoner for Louisville. Word had gotten out about the suspect, and the Bowling Green authorities had to breach a crowd of more than one thousand to get their prisoner to the depot and depart for Louisville. However, on the train's arrival in Louisville in the wee hours of the morning on June 6, Major Ridge and Lieutenant Dave McElliott boarded the train at Fourth avenue and A street, before its arrival at Union Station, on Tenth and Broadway. They planned to see and speak to the man before the train pulled into the station. The Bowling Green authorities transporting the prisoner were also met by Chief Lindsey and Benedict Thomas, the latter presumably to make an identification, but the man was quickly confirmed to not be Wendling. Despite the early hour, a large crowd gathered at the station and proved difficult for the police to control. Presumably, Smith was returned to Bowling Green that same day, not in custody.

On the afternoon of June 5, some excitement arose in Louisville when it was learned that the police had made a long trip, having inquired if there was sufficient fuel in a vehicle to go thirty miles. The trip, however, was never mentioned again. Information had been received that certain people who knew Wendling had heard him say he was going back to France if he could raise enough money. With Wendling still being sought, two thousand circulars were printed, half in French and half in German. They were in the process of being dispatched to every quarter of the globe, with the assistance of the U.S. State Department.

The first Sunday High Mass following the discovery of the body was celebrated at 10:00 a.m. on June 5 by Father Schuhmann. The church was, as might be expected, full, and there was much anxious waiting for what the priest would have to say about the murder.

Father Schuhmann started with reading 1 Peter, verse 6.

> *Dearly Beloved: Be you humbled under the mighty hand of God, that He may exact you in the time of visitation. Casting all your care upon Him, for He hath care of you. Be sober and watch, because your adversary, the devil, as a roaring lion, goeth about seeking whom he may devour. Whom resist ye, strong in faith; knowing that the same affliction befalls your brethren who are in the world. But the God of all grace, who hath called us unto his eternal glory in Christ Jesus, after you have suffered a little, will Himself perfect you, and confirm you, and establish you. To Him be glory and empire for ever and ever.*

He continued with the Gospel of St. Luke, verses 1–10.

> *At that time the publicans and sinners drew near unto Jesus to hear Him. And the Pharisees and the Scribes murmured, saying: "This man receiveth sinners and eateth with them." And He spoke to them this parable, saying: "What man is there of you that hath a hundred sheep; and if he shall lose one of them doth he not leave the ninety-nine in the desert and go after that which is lost until he find it? And when he hath found it, lay it upon his shoulder rejoicing, and coming home call together his friends and neighbors, saying to them; "Rejoice with me because I have found my sheep that was lost." I say to you that even so there shall be joy in heaven upon one sinner that doth penance more than upon ninety-nine just who need not penance. Or that woman having ten groats if she lose one groat doth not light a candle and sweep the house and seek diligently until she find it? And when she has found it call together her friends and neighbors, saying: "Rejoice with me, because I have found the groat which I had lost." So I say to you, there shall be joy before the angels of God upon one sinner doing penance.*

He finished the reading, quoting again from the epistle of St. Peter: "Be you humbled under the mighty hand of God, that He may exalt you in the time of visitation, casting all your care upon Him, for He hath care of you." Although this was, in fact, the epistle and gospel to be read on the third Sunday after Pentecost every year, at every Catholic Mass, it "touched indirectly upon the tribulation which has visited the congregation of St. John's Church." Father Schuhmann counseled his listeners to "be of good faith, to be patient under the weight of adverse criticism and to trust in God to give them courage to bear up under deplorable circumstances which have cast a shadow over the parish." He did not, however, directly mention Alma Kellner, although she was certainly on his mind and the mind of every congregant in the sanctuary.

Dr. Edmund B. Patterson, of the Trinity Methodist Church on Third and Guthrie streets, however, was more forthcoming. In a sermon on Sunday evening, entitled "Some Lessons for Us in the Alma Kellner Case," he drew upon the text "The wages of sin is death, but the gift of God is eternal life." He declared that "if Wendling did the deed he can't get away from God." He reviewed the circumstances of the murder with his congregation, noting that if the body was that of Alma Kellner, as it was presumed to be, she was in a far better place and her "little spirit was not touched." He avowed that she had been enjoying eternal life since her death the previous December.

The parade of suspects being arrested across the United States continued to grow. A man called S.C. Whaley was apprehended in Williamson, West Virginia, suspected of criminal assaults on eight little girls, but he denied being Wendling. (He was, it was noted, already subject to execution for the crimes he had committed in West Virginia.) Indianapolis, Indiana police were also on the lookout, searching all places in the city where Wendling might be hiding.

Finally, on June 8, the inquest was to be held. It had been delayed a second time because Dr. Robins was completing his work. Aaron Kohn, a well-known local attorney who was thought to be retained to represent the Kellner family at the inquest, was said to be familiarizing himself with the facts and visiting the church. Kohn was given an escort of the church premises by Frank Fehr, Dr. Duncan and Deputy Coroner Kammerer. Dr. Robins concluded that the stains found on Wendling's clothing, retrieved from his room, were human blood and confirmed that an attempt had been made to burn Alma Kellner's body. His report would stand in lieu of his appearance at the inquest, and it was understood that Dr. Robins was to leave Louisville that day to go on his long-overdue vacation.

A large crowd had gathered the day before in the courthouse basement, near the door to the coroner's office, at the time the inquest was initially scheduled and had been disappointed by the delay. It was believed that Lena Wendling would be arraigned in police court on the morning of June 8, as well, but since the same witnesses would be needed at both her arraignment and the inquest, it was presumed that her arraignment would be delayed again. It was still hoped that the "woman in black" who had seen Alma Kellner at the altar rail would come forward. Richard Sweet was present at the coroner's office, appearing pale, and told newspaper reporters "he had not been able to retain anything on his stomach since he unearthed the body." He confirmed, however, that he had put in a claim for the reward money, which would be decided by the general council. It was also revealed publicly that a letter had been found in the Wendlings' room at the rectory addressed to Edward Wendling, Joseph's father, in France. It was written in French and signed by Lena and was presumably part of the packet of correspondence that had reportedly been found.

During the evening hours of June 8, the "last link in the chain of evidence which goes to show that Alma Kellner reached St. John's church" that morning was furnished when the woman in black at last made herself known. Mrs. Rosa Stauble called Frank Fehr at his store, leaving a message for him. She telephoned him at about 6:00 p.m., and he was contacted about the call just as he was going to dinner at the Seelbach. She told Fehr that she was the woman who had sat with a Mrs. Grahle at St. John's Church. Fehr hurried to her home, and she related her story to him, stating that she had remained in the church after the other women had left to pray for a few moments in solitude. She saw the janitor emerge from the sacristy and glance at the child several times. He was pretending to be "inspecting something at the altar." He came out and walked down the aisle of the church closest to Clay street and went to the folding doors in the back. She was somewhat suspicious and watched as he returned from the vestibule and went back to the altar. She left the church at about 10:45 a.m., arriving at her home on nearby Marshall street at about 11:00 a.m.

Fehr immediately reported the interview to Chief Lindsey and Dr. Duncan, and Mrs. Stauble was expected to be summoned to the inquest. Fehr expressed dismay that it had taken so long to get the information; he knew that Father Schuhmann had spoken to his congregation about the need to come forward with any information. However, the two women were not members of St. John's Church, having only attended Mass that day at the church out of convenience for the feast day and presumably learned of the need to come forward through other means.

The first morning of the inquest, held in the coroner's office in the courthouse, was taken up with selecting the jury. Finally, six were seated: John L. Dunlap, stock and bond broker; James B. Camp, restaurant proprietor; Charles A. Shaw, manager of the Masonic Theater; A.H. Cooper, real

The Commonwealth of Kentucky, Jefferson Circuit Court, Criminal Branch, June Term, A.D. 1910—
The Commonwealth of Kentucky vs. Joseph Wendling.

The grand jury of the county of Jefferson, in the name and by the authority of the Commonwealth of Kentucky, accuse Joseph Wendling of the crime of willful murder, committed in manner and form as follows, to-wit:

That the said Joseph Wendling, in the said county of Jefferson, on the 8th day of December, 1909, and before the finding of this indictment, in and upon one Alma Kellner, a female infant person, unlawfully, willfully, feloniously, maliciously and of his malice aforethought, did make an assault, and he, the said Joseph Wendling, in some way and manner, and by some means, instruments and weapons to the grand jurors unknown, did then and there unlawfully, willfully, feloniously, maliciously and of his malice aforethought, kill and murder the said Alma Kellner, so that and whereby she, Alma Kellner, did then and there die, and so the grand jurors aforesaid say that the said Joseph Wendling, in the manner and by the means aforesaid, to them, the said grand jurors, unknown, did then and there unlawfully, willfully, maliciously, feloniously and of his malice aforethought, kill and murder her, the said Alma Kellner, contrary to the form of the statutes in such cases made and provided against the peace and dignity of the Commonwealth of Kentucky.

6
THE DRAGNET

As the grand jury dawdled, and with Captain Carney already heading to Texas in search of Joseph Wendling, the police chief determined to wait no longer. Chief Lindsey went to Clerk Harry C. Nehan of the police court and swore out an affidavit as to the facts pointing to Wendling's guilt. With that, an arrest warrant was issued. The information was immediately sent to Frankfort in order for the governor to issue the requisition—the paperwork necessary to request that the Texas governor assist Louisville in capturing Wendling, who was believed to be in that state. It was noted that the name of the officer who was to take Wendling into custody was not indicated on the document and would have to be filled in. The material was sent immediately to Carney, and it was presumed that the Texas governor, Thomas Mitchell Campbell, would honor it, especially since the grand jury would presumably follow up with an indictment in short order. When asked, Chief Lindsey expressed confidence that, this time, the correct man had been identified and Wendling would soon be in custody.

When the indictment was returned, another warrant was prepared and communicated to Captain Carney, already on a train to Texas, having set out in search of Joseph Wendling. On June 21, 1910, it was reported on the front page of the *Courier-Journal* that Wendling was under surveillance by authorities in Houston. Carney was reportedly already reaching Houston, and it was revealed that he had in hand a requisition to Governor Thomas Mitchell Campbell, from Governor A.E. Willson, demanding the return of

Joseph Wendling. This would need to be taken not to Houston, however, but to Austin, the state capital of Texas. When the indictment was issued, along with the accompanying arrest warrant, and "flashed over the wire" to Carney, he was prepared to take immediate action. On the evening of June 20, a telegram was received that the Texas governor had yet to receive the papers but that he would be waiting for the requisition in order to give Captain Carney the legal ability to receive the assistance of Texas authorities in apprehending Wendling.

In explaining how Captain Carney came to be in Texas, it was finally revealed that the Louisville Police Department had received a tip on June 13 from a Texas officer that he had located Wendling working at a ranch outside Houston and that he could turn him over as soon as he had the proper legal paperwork. It was later made known that, in fact, the original tip came to Chief George Ellis of Houston from a farmhand who had become acquainted with Wendling during his time in Texas. Chief Lindsey began his own investigation, but the Texas chief was very close-mouthed, not wishing to risk the reward or run afoul of Texas law regarding the capture of suspected felons. (Under Texas law, he could not seize Wendling until he held in his hands the warrant from his own governor.) Ellis remained in communication with Lindsey while they waited for the grand jury to return the indictment and also remained in contact with the farmhand, who had returned to the farm to continue working and to keep an eye on Wendling.

Chief Lindsey, however, did not stop working the case in Louisville and was finally able to obtain another photo of Wendling, one that was considered better than the old photograph of him in his French army uniform. He had haunted all the locations where Wendling had been in the habit of frequenting and found a photo in a West End saloon that was purported to be of Wendling.

The newspaper noted that the exact route of Wendling's return, once apprehended, would be a carefully guarded secret and would not be announced until he was safely inside the Jefferson County Jail.

It was remarked that word was being sent, post haste, to Captain Carney so that Wendling could be promptly apprehended. In a bit of pique for being excluded from such a big story, the newspaper noted that "for some reason, the Louisville officers tried to keep secret the fact that a requisition has been issued for Wendling to return to Kentucky." The reporter indicated that Governor Willson kept the secret but that the information was obtained in an indirect way by a correspondent and later confirmed by checking with the governor's office, "where the papers are on file and are public records." What they could not determine, however, was where Wendling actually was, since all that was required for the requisition was the name of the state.

The process, as it was described in the newspaper, was for the agent (Captain Carney) to go to the governor of Texas and have issued a Texas warrant for the arrest. At that time, the Texas governor would be informed of the location of Joseph Wendling, as known to Carney. The next day, with a dateline of Houston, it was revealed that Chief Ellis of Houston, along with Carney, the chief of detectives for Louisville, were "speeding across Texas" toward an unknown western destination. Their trail led them through San Antonio toward the Mexican border, as they believed Wendling was headed that way. The Houston chief of detectives, William Kessler, had worked with Carney and indicated that they were positive of his identification. It was expected that the pair would return to Houston with Wendling the next day.

Chief Lindsey worked assiduously in Louisville, stating to reporters that he had not had a good meal or night's sleep during the process. He remained at his office until after midnight, leaving Major Patrick Ridge, the night chief, with instructions to notify him at once of any concerns. They would be notified by long-distance phone of the capture when it occurred. That did not happen as expected, however, and Carney and Ellis returned to Houston by train. Carney's aim was to get "one view" of Wendling, who he believed he would be able to immediately recognize. The concern was that too much publicity would alert Wendling, who was reportedly west of San Antonio, more than three hundred miles away. Unfortunately, when they arrived, with Deputy Sheriff J.M. Long (San Antonio County), at Dullnig farm some eight miles east of San Antonio, where Wendling had been working, they learned that he had left the day before. They were able to confirm with the San Antonio police chief Van Riper and Sheriff Lindsey of that county that the man matched Wendling's description exactly.

Back in Houston, the Harris County sheriff, Archie Anderson, and Chief Ellis had previously "stoutly maintained" that Wendling was not in custody but confirmed that they knew that a man of his description had been spotted. Captain Carney had arrived several days before, and only local law enforcement authorities knew of his presence in the city. He did not register at any local hotel and was only recognized by newspapermen who knew him from Louisville. Once they returned, Carney sent a brief telegram to Chief Lindsey: "Returned from ranch. Party left day before yesterday. Still have lead. J.P.C." The chief expected that this would be followed by a more detailed special-delivery letter describing what had happened.

Joseph Wendling had once again slipped away. Captain Carney stayed in Texas for a few days, trying to locate Wendling with the help of the Texas authorities. The Mexican police were also notified and given information. Secretary Knox of the U.S. State Department assured Lindsey that the Mexican government had agreed that "nothing will be left undone to capture Wendling if he has fled to that country."

A man strongly resembling Wendling was arrested on June 24 but was released when it was confirmed that he was "only a tramp."

Captain Carney remained on the trail. The *Houston Post* reported on June 28 that "membership in the Wendling Suspect club is increasing rapidly," with two more men being arrested in Galveston and Waco due to their resemblance to the circulated photos of Wendling. Carney was being kept busy inspecting the various suspects. In the case of the Galveston suspect, the sheriff, S.J. Winston, felt quite confident that he had the right man. Among other tests, they instructed the man to write his name (which he rendered as "Josofo Wendeling") and declared that it matched the facsimile copy of Wendling's signature. At the same time, Constable O.L. Birchfield of Moody insisted that he had the right man in Waco. Both detained men denied being Joseph Wendling, and in the end, both were found to be speaking the truth.

It was later reported that, as the trail wound its way throughout the country, Captain Carney tracked Wendling into Mexico and Central America, specifically Panama, at one point. Captain Carney had received tips that suggested both places as possible destinations for the missing man.

On a side note, on June 23, the *Courier-Journal* reported that it was rumored that Richard Sweet had been discharged from his employment. Jacob Haller, connected with the firm, denied that, stating that Sweet had been employed as a laborer and been allowed several days off to assist the police in the investigation. After a week, they asked him to return to work, and he was expected back on June 8. However, he did not return. Sweet was told to come in on June 9, but he explained that he was testifying before the coroner's inquest—in fact, he probably was. The firm then employed another man. Sweet, however, claimed that he was sick as a result of the horrific discovery and unable to work and that the plumbing firm had simply fired him.

As the chase went on, presumed sightings of Wendling occurred around the globe. In late July, a report indicated that he was believed to be in Italy, and Italian detectives, spurred by the thought of a reward, made a strong effort to trace him to their country. They were unsuccessful, however.

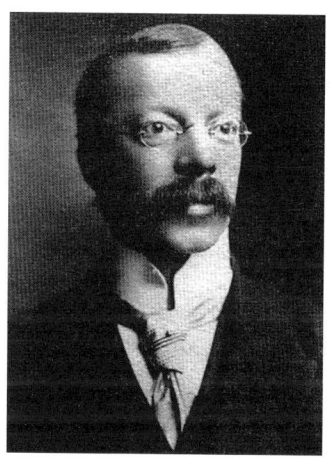

Dr. Hawley Harvey Crippen, the *Daily Mirror*, August 1, 1910. *Courtesy of the* London Daily Mirror.

While all eyes were seeking Wendling, the world was also caught up in another high-profile chase. Across the Atlantic Ocean, Dr. Hawley Crippen and his lover, Ethel Leneve, were suspects in the death of Crippen's wife, Belle Elmore, in London earlier that spring. Belle was last seen on January 31, 1910. Crippen, spooked by the attention of the London police to the disappearance, fled England, which further interested the London police. After multiple searches of the home they shared, a torso was found and identified by a scar.

The lovers were passengers on a steamship, the *Montrose*, which was headed for Canada. Through stories in newspapers across the globe, the entire world knew that the pair were being sought and would be apprehended when they reached Canadian waters. The only persons who did not know of the chase were the couple themselves, on a ship in the Atlantic Ocean with no means of communication with the outside world. For the first time, via the wireless telegraph, the apprehension was being choreographed through the ship's crew. Crippen and Leneve were kept unawares of their situation by the ship's officers. It was a race to learn whether Wendling or Crippen would be captured first.

On Sunday, July 31, 1910, the *Montrose* entered Canadian waters and was met by a pilot boat. On board was the Scotland Yard inspector Water Dew, who had caught a faster ship and passed the *Montrose*. He placed the pair under arrest, and they were returned to England, where, ultimately, Crippen was executed for the murder. Leneve was eventually set free, having been found to have no knowledge of the actual murder.

7
THE CAPTURE

Finally, on July 31, 1910, the Sunday morning headline of the *Courier-Journal* flashed the news: "Wendling Run Down by Carney; Denied Killing Alma Kellner; Arrest Made in San Francisco." Captain Carney's message to the newspaper, dated July 30, stated: "San Francisco, July 30.—The Courier-Journal, Louisville: We have got Joseph Wendling here. He admits his identity and recognized me. I had quite a little conversation with him. He waives papers. I have wired Chief of Police Lindsey and am awaiting his reply. I will probably start for home just as soon as I can get rested up." It was signed, "John P. Carney, Chief of Detectives, Louisville."

After a chase that took him through a half dozen states of the Union, through Mexico and a portion of Central America, Carney had tracked Wendling to San Francisco. Captain Carney had received information that California authorities had traced the fugitive to a house in San Francisco. He had also reportedly been spotted some two weeks before, in Vallejo, living under an assumed name. Chief William T. Stanford of that city was on alert, but Wendling became aware that he was under suspicion and fled.

The actual arrest was anticlimactic, with Wendling dragged from underneath a sink in a boardinghouse washroom by detectives Thomas P. Burke and George H. Ryan of the San Francisco Police Department. Wendling had been staying in a lodging house that was kept by Mary Moriarty, at 362 Third street. The two officers had watched the place the previous afternoon and set out on the morning of July 30 to make

WENDLING RUN DOWN BY CARNEY; DENIES KILLING ALMA KELLNER; ARREST MADE IN SAN FRANCISCO

Woman Frenchman Had Wooed and Won Gave the Tip To Louisville Chief At Hume, Mo.

Headline in the *Courier-Journal*, July 17, 1910.

the arrest. With Ryan covering the rear, Burke sought entry at the front, over Moriarty's objections. Burke persisted and finally located Wendling, recognizing him immediately from the photograph, although he had shaved off his mustache. Wendling readily admitted his identity. Initially, the two officers believed that Moriarty knew he was a fugitive and was trying to hide him, but she explained that she simply thought "he might have gotten in some little difficulty over 'mashing girls at a nickelodeon,'" and she wanted to spare him the consequences. She claimed to have had no idea that her tenant was wanted on such a serious matter and was very contrite when she learned of it.

Captain Carney had learned of the arrest while on a train just a few miles outside of San Francisco, from a newspaper story that reported the arrest that day. He immediately proceeded to meet the local police and to finally set eyes on the man he had been tracking for so many weeks and miles.

With Wendling caught, it was revealed that his fate was finally sealed by information provided by one Cora Munea. She had first met Wendling at her aunt's home in Houston, and the widow was dazzled by the "dashing young Frenchman." He had wooed her with tales of the wealth he would have when his aged father in France died. They allegedly became engaged to be married, but before she returned to her home, in Hume, Missouri, she had come to fear him. She knew him as Henry Jacquemin, the name he had used in his perambulations across the country. He had been trailed as well by the letters and postcards he had sent to "women friends," most of whom were of the "dissolute class." Munea, however, was the exception;

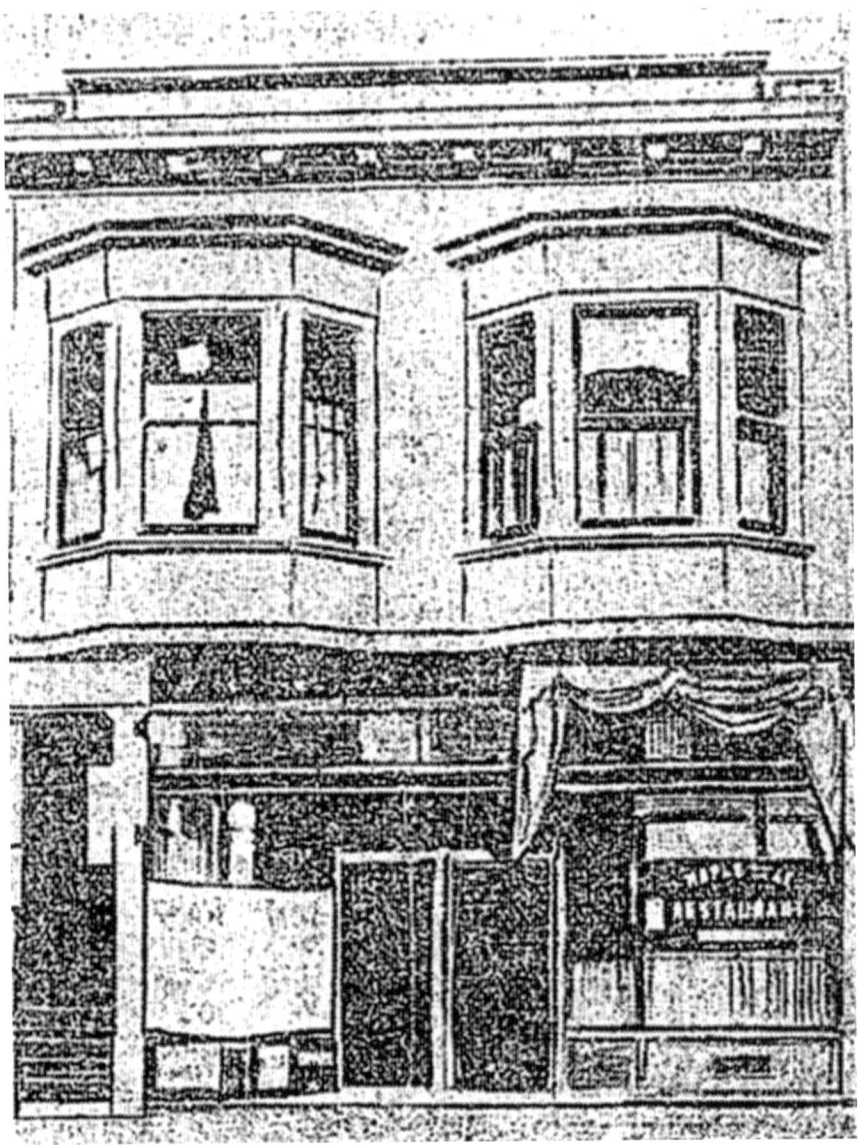

"Boardinghouse Run by Mary Moriarty, in San Francisco," published in the *Courier-Journal*.

she was the "only respectable woman" connected to Wendling during the spring and summer, and she worked as a milliner in Missouri.

Working with Munea, Captain Carney had sent a "decoy letter" to Wendling, using his assumed name of Jacquemin, and learned that he had passed through Los Angeles. Another clue came when Wendling sent a postal card in May to a friend in San Antonio from Rio Vista, California, written in French, reporting that he had gotten a job for ten dollars a week and board. Carney had followed up on that lead with the help of cooperative local authorities, but they lost the lead. With that, Carney had gone to Hume, Missouri, and reported a "hard trip" there, having been "delayed by washouts and slides." He "rode forty-nine miles into Kansas on the tailend of a freight train." He was rewarded by seeing a postcard from Vallejo dated April 5, from "H.J."

Chief Eugene R. Wall detailed the San Francisco end of the investigation. He noted that Captain Carney had communicated with him on July 23 that Wendling had worked at a Vallejo location. He learned that Wendling had left there but tracked him down working as a gardener for Charles Wiedmann. While working there, the man being sought had "made himself objectionable to the servant maid" and left. Also while in Vallejo, he allegedly committed several burglaries and stole items from a home owned by Naval Constructor Saudners[8] and gave the items to a "dancing girl" named Alice Miller. He left that area in May, returned and then left again.

Captain Carney expressed his highest praise for the San Francisco officers, Chief Martin and Captain Wall, and the two detectives who made the arrest. He extolled the degree of cooperation he'd received from them. He agreed that he was happy the chase was over and "if you had traveled as far as I have you would be happy, too." With his man safely behind bars, Carney stated his plan was to head back as "soon as I have a little sleep and wash up."

It was remarked by the newspaper that Captain Carney had stayed on the trail for two months and covered nearly eleven thousand miles. He had his reward at noon on July 30, when he walked into the city prison with Captain Wall and confirmed that, at last, he had Wendling in his sight. Wendling asked, "You're Chief Carney?" when he arrived. Carney affirmed that he was.

Given the chance to talk to local newspapermen, Wendling denied his guilt emphatically. He hinted that his predecessor at the church, a man whose name he claimed not to remember, had access to the basement. (Of course, he was in fact acquainted with Benedict Thomas, who had continued living at the church after leaving his position as janitor; presumably, Wendling saw him regularly.) He claimed not to know he was being sought until three weeks before, when he read about the money being offered and "laughed at the idea of the reward." Wendling explained his precipitous departure in

January as being the result of trouble with his wife—the "thrifty one of the family." He claimed she took all his earnings and he "no get enough for cigar or glass beer." He took his mother's maiden name, Jacquemin, to hide from his wife. He even had an explanation for the bloodstained clothes, claiming to have shot himself in the hand with a revolver about that same time and "there was a lot of blood."

The Vallejo police, in the meantime, believed that Wendling was involved in several burglaries of a house owned by "a woman of the Vallejo underworld named Alice Miller or Alice Roberts." Wendling admitted knowing her but denied that he'd committed a burglary. Following his arrest, the police found in Wendling's possession a number of items taken from the home, as well as photos and letters from a number of women. Men who had lodged with him knew little about him but mentioned that he "talked familiarly about women."

After his arrest, it was reported that his movements had been tracked in the area for some days and that the two arresting officers had worked hard on the case. It was while Captain Carney was in Missouri, conferring with Cora Munea, that he learned of the lead to Vallejo and why he had immediately headed back to California.

Chief Carney also spoke at length about the manhunt to the local newspapermen, who shared the story back to the home newspaper. His "odyssey of duty" led him over thousands of miles, tracking Wendling. He described how they initially believed Kellner might have been kidnapped, and it "never left the minds" of both the chief and himself that "a degenerate had done away with the child." He led a long and detailed search of every sewer, outhouse and basement within a few miles of the church. He described the theory of the crime as follows:

> *The way the body was concealed was this: The furnace of St. John's church is in the basement and is reached by a passageway cut through the clay bank foundation. The man strangled the girl in the church and dragged her body into the basement and placed it on the top of the clay bank under the floor of the church. He left it there until it began to decompose. Then he considered burning it and evidently tried to force it into the furnace, but he must have feared that the odor would carry and changed that plan. Then he wrapped the body in an old carpet and covered it with ashes and carried it 300 feet to a spot under a music room. He buried it under two feet of earth. When the floods came the place filled with water and the priest had the space pumped out. The plumber discovered the body on May 30.*

Back at home, the arrest was greeted with great relief. Frank Fehr expressed "his opinion that the closing chapter in the famous case is now being written." He expressed confidence that Wendling was guilty but noted that if he was not, he "was sure that the law will treat him fairly and give him the benefit of that doubt, whatever it may be." Fehr commended the tireless work of Captain Carney in capturing Wendling. Alma Kellner's parents had little public comment, although it was noted that Mrs. Kellner had suffered a complete collapse when her daughter's body was found. She had been confined to her bed in a critical condition and for the two months since had been under the constant care of a physician.

It was also learned that, while in San Francisco, Colonel James P. Whallen, along with his friend A. Scott Bullitt, while on an "extended pleasure tour of the West," had spent several days with Carney at the end of the hunt. He had telegraphed back to his brother, Colonel John H. Whallen, and the local police about the possibility of an arrest soon.

One of the telegrams filed with the Western Union Telegraph office in San Francisco read as follows: "San Francisco, Cal., June 29, 1910[9]—Col. John H. Whallen, Buckingham, Theater, Louisville, Ky. Jack has nailed the prize and will leave with 'W' via Chicago. Tip 'W.O.' to have plenty of men at depot, so as to prevent any trouble and possibly a riot. Let nothing leak. Jack P. Whallen."

It was noted that "W" was, of course, Wendling and "W.O" was William O. Head, Louisville's mayor. Colonel John Whallen, in turn, shared the news with the "highest city authorities." He assisted in arranging for Wendling's return to avoid the possibly of a riot, or even lynching, upon their arrival. Telegrams that followed urged that a cordon of "picked men" be placed at the depot prior to the train's appearance at the station. Whallen also expressed his praise for the San Francisco police and, of course, for Carney, who, he stated, was "one of the very best natural detectives he had ever met."

On August 3, 1910, at 9:00 a.m., Wendling left San Francisco on the train with Carney and, it was reported, "with a smile." He left the prisoner manacled to Detective Thomas Burke and was escorted to the train on a streetcar, then on a ferry steamer, to board the Oakland train, by Detectives George Ryan and Thomas Maloney, as well. Wendling took his leave of Chief of Police Martin with a handshake and appeared carefree. As they reached the ferry, Wendling spotted a flower booth with a vase of American Beauty roses and asked Detective Burke to purchase him a flower. Burke did so, placing the rose in Wendling's lapel. It was expected that Chief Lindsey

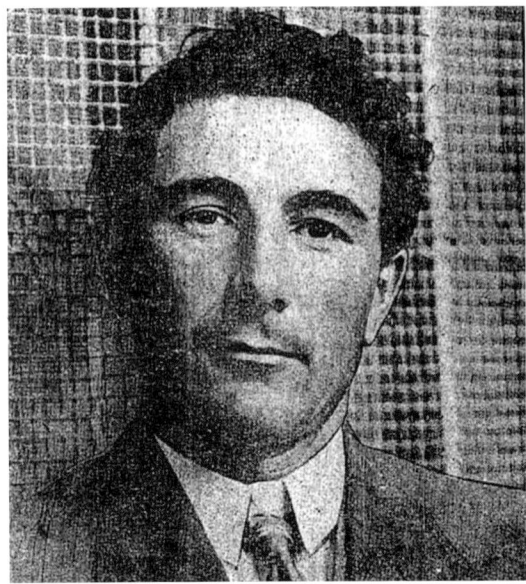

Joseph Wendling, photo taken shortly after his arrest in San Francisco, as published in the *Courier-Journal*.

and Colonel John Whallen would meet the party at Denver. Before Wendling left the California jail, Chief Martin had Bertillon measurements[10] taken of Wendling's skull and noted that the "only surprising feature developed...was the fine physique of the man, which is the exception rather than the rule with human misfits whose manner and mode of life are conducive to frail bodies and flabby muscles." Wendling did, however, have an "unusual large lobe of the ear, indicative of the criminal and the degenerate," as well as a "short, protruding nose lying between close-set eyes."

Of course, the media trailed Wendling as he returned to Louisville, reporting on his every move and comment along the way. From Denver, Colorado, it was reported that Wendling "let slip to-day the first statement that can be regarded as a damaging admission, indicating that he never saw the Kellner girl, agreeing that 'no doubt she came there,'" but there were so many girls and he didn't know "one from the other." He did recall assisting Father Schuhmann with searching the church after her disappearance but that they "did not look in the place where the body was discovered." Realizing the significance of what he said, however, he quickly followed up, stating that he did not know where the body was discovered but that they "could not have looked there, otherwise we should have found it." It was mentioned that during their stopover in Denver, during which time Wendling was locked up in the Denver jail, the reporters were given free access to him. Carney, when asked, claimed to expect no trouble getting him back to

Louisville but that they were prepared to slip him into the city "carefully and quietly" nonetheless. Chief Lindsey was equally reticent, noting that Carney still needed sleep and that they would not leave until he was ready.

The reporters observed that the "volatile Frenchman [was] in a continued gale of merriment." He was quite willing to talk of himself, but when questions about the crime arose, Wendling "failed to understand English, and when they were repeated in French, answered guardedly." He considered the accusations against him to be a "huge joke." He claimed his departure was due to the nagging of his wife and his brother-in-law and that he was sorry he'd married her. They'd only gone to Louisville, in fact, because her brother Alois was already living there. He expressed his only fear to be meeting his wife again and that the thought caused "the shivers run up and down my back." However, he soon expressed happiness that his wife acknowledged that it was her fault that Wendling had left and that she had already hired an attorney to represent him. It was noted that she was deserted by him and that, since his arrest, he had not been the slightest curious as to her welfare. Instead, he'd spent his time boasting of his conquests during his travels.

Lena Wendling, in the meantime, had secured the services of J. Reginald Clements, a Louisville defense attorney. When Clements was asked about his representation of Wendling, he agreed that he was likely going to accept the request to serve as counsel for him. With respect to Clements's fees, according to Lena Wendling, an anonymous man had assured her that "money would be forthcoming" to pay for Joseph Wendling's defense. Likewise, Alois Arnold had agreed that while he hadn't been on good terms with his brother-in-law, he bore him no malice and would do everything possible to assist him. He didn't believe he would be permitted to see him, however, as he hadn't been allowed to see his sister when she was incarcerated. Lena also notified her parents-in-law in France that her husband had been found and taken into custody.

Carney, when questioned about the trip so far, remarked that Wendling had behaved admirably and had even complimented Carney on his own "good nature." He had only let Wendling out of his sight when he knew him to be securely behind bars. During the stopover in Denver, he and Lindsey "devoted most of the day to riding about the city and suburbs with city officers," having decided against "sweating" Wendling on the trip. It was later revealed that Captain Carney was not feeling well and that Chief Lindsey had wanted to spend more time in Denver to give Carney an opportunity to rest. But Carney insisted on continuing, as he wanted to be home if he became even more seriously ill.

The men left Denver on August 7, with their next stop planned to be Kansas City. They were traveling in the stateroom of the Pullman sleeper train the *Nautilus*. The trio accompanying Wendling, along with Denver officers, had supposedly "sweated" him for some two hours in an attempt to "trip him into a confession." Wendling readily answered queries about the day in question but was able to avoid any incriminating response. He agreed that twice he and Father Schuhmann had noted an odd odor from the furnace but had been unable to find anything that might have caused it. Lindsey agreed that Wendling maintained a cheerful disposition, "which appears absolutely genuine and not faked." It was claimed that Wendling did not know that Lindsey was the police chief and that, when he first met Carney, he apparently assumed that he was the Louisville police chief. He was set right by a Louisville newspaper correspondent. Chief Armstrong of the Denver Police Department told reporters that "he is either innocent or he has a marvelously shrewd mind and a wonderful memory. If he is guilty he has fixed indelibly on his mind every statement he has made in San Francisco and here since his arrest, and he cannot be led into blunders over them."

Wendling was taken in a police patrol car to the station, handcuffed to Captain Carney. There he was the "center of all eyes," laughing, joking and smoking cigarettes. He waved to reporters on the platform and reminded them that he was "an innocent man." He did, however, recognize that the "public sentiment [was] strongly against" him, given that the police were doing everything in their power to convict him. Wendling expressed confidence that his friends, who had raised money for his defense, would not allow him to be railroaded during his trial. During the wait for the train, he smiled broadly and "even consented to make it more expansive at the request of photographers." It was reported that there was little chance of Wendling escaping given that he remained handcuffed to Carney, who was considerably larger than Wendling—the handcuffs made it very much like he was chained to a stone wall.

In Kansas City, Cora Munea arrived to wait for the train coming from the west. As she had provided the tip that led to Wendling's arrest, she intended to see about claiming part of the reward for his capture. She conferred with Wentworth E. Griffin, the local police chief. Although an attempt was made to prevent her from being spotted and recognized, news quickly spread that "one of the most important characters connected with the famous Kellner case" was at the station; a crowd quickly gathered. Munea, being a practical businesswoman, used the opportunity of a trip to a large city to do her fall buying for her millinery business. She explained that her business had been harmed by her connection to the case.

It was expected that there would be only a brief stopover, some twenty minutes, in Kansas City, before the train moved on to St. Louis. That would give her an opportunity to meet with Captain Carney and the others. She would be accompanied by Chief Wentworth E. Griffin and Inspector Ed P. Boyle. She stated that she would hire a Louisville attorney to represent her interests there, if necessary, but that she was sure that Carney would see that she was fairly treated. She considered him "not only one of the greatest detectives in this country" but also "one of the nicest men" she had ever met. Joseph Wendling, she stated, was "nothing" to her.

Cora Munea (spelled "Munes" in the article), it was reported, very much gave the impression of a successful businesswoman. Since she was in the fashion business, it was noted that she "wore a neat cream colored dress with little or no trimming," with a straw hat of the same color that was "set off by a large white plume."

Another reward claimant came forward. Joe Tamborella of Houston claimed that he provided the first clue that indicated Wendling was using the name Jacquemin in Texas. He had seen the photographs on the wanted poster and one of the postcard photographs Joseph Wendling was fond of sharing. Tamborella had tipped off Chief Ellis and was joined with the chief in claiming a reward for the information.

The next leg of the trip was to be short, from Kansas City to St. Louis. As they rolled ever closer to Louisville, Wendling began to lose the bravado he had shown during the trip. "After hours of relentless 'sweating' in a stateroom cell on the Pullman," he no longer responded to questions with a smile. Even on a fast mail train, the Union Pacific, it took some eight hours to travel across Missouri. They were met in St. Louis by a large crowd, at least one thousand curious people, but police were prepared, and the scene was orderly. The train was stopped just outside of town, where Chief Griffin and Inspector Boyle boarded to confer with their Louisville colleagues. They were allowed to see Joseph Wendling, as were reporters and photographers waiting at the station. While Wendling was posing for the reporters, at the station in Kansas City, Cora Munea met with Captain Carney and was "told of some startling declarations Wendling had made concerning her character….Then and there Mrs. Munea resolved to confront the prisoner" and was allowed to board the train for the trip to St. Louis. However, Wendling did not know she was onboard. The "sweating"—the third degree—re-commenced when they

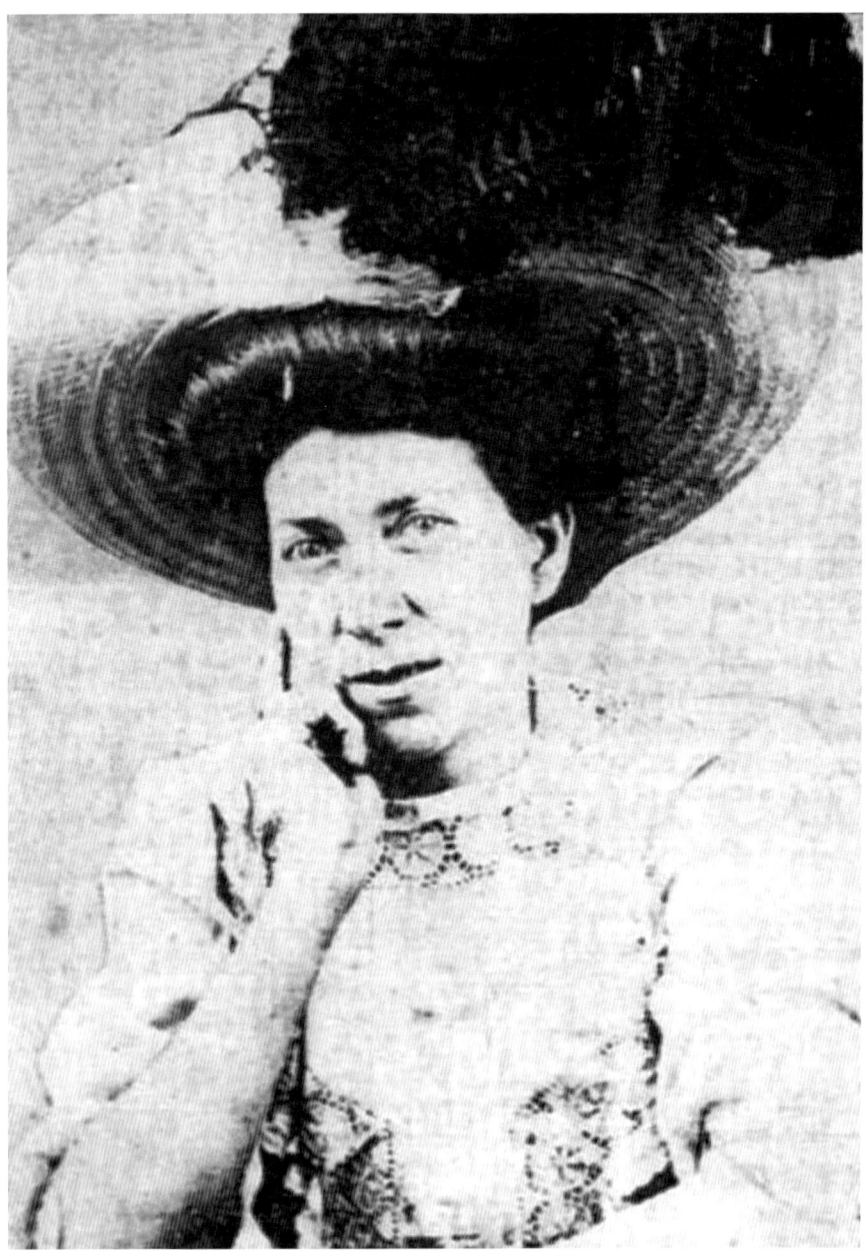

Cora Munea. *Courtesy of* St. Louis Post-Dispatch.

left the station, with Chief Lindsey taking over. In the "sweatbox," the "grilling began in earnest." Wendling continued to throw the blame for the murder on Benedict Thomas. When faced with the statement that he alone had the keys, he suggested that perhaps Thomas had gotten in and stolen them. He continued to claim that the clothing that had been found, stained with blood, was the result of an accidental shooting he'd suffered earlier. (Chief Lindsey at one point told him that the blood had been found to be "female blood," which of course could not be determined with the science of the time.)

Wendling complained: "You treat me mean, no give me my dinner, you no let me shave or perfume my hair or powder my face to-day. You treat me mean. You think me sick, I am hungry all the time."

Wendling denied having said in San Francisco that "if he were guilty no one but God would know of it." In response, Carney called him a liar. Wendling continued to dodge questions and demanded a drink of water.

Also on the train with the party was Dr. Albert Ross Hill, the president of Missouri State University at Columbia. Dr. Hill was considered one of the greatest authorities on psychology in the United States and was invited to observe the sweating and serve, in part, as a witness that Wendling was not being abused. Hill told a newspaper: "This is one of the most wonderful cases of abnormal development I have ever seen. This chap is just a bundle of nerves, and although they have stood him in good stead so far, I believe that the end is about at hand. I feel that when he does weaken he will suffer a complete collapse and you will hear a story that will startle even those most intimately connected with the case."

He cautioned, however:

> *That he is an abnormal chap there is no question, and his actions would lead me to believe that he is guilty of the crime. However, it would be unfair for me to judge him before he is legally tried. This is simply an expert opinion based on what I saw in that room. The chap could not answer any direct question and invariably resorted to a subterfuge to dodge the question. It was an impossibility to hold his eyes, while he closely observed everyone gathered about him. His eyes were constantly dancing. When we started in he laughed many of the questions off, but toward the close this smile had changed to a nervous twitching beneath the skin. Oh, yes, he will soon break down and I would advise that the most careful watch be kept on him.*

Taking that advice to heart, Lindsey ordered that the handcuffs stay on for the remainder of the trip. This irritated Wendling, but he "ate freely of the lunch provided for him" and smoked, while the officers prepared to "sweat" him for the second time that day. This would be his fifth session of questioning.

Wendling, unwisely, commented that he had spoken the truth about Cora Munea and that the officers were "afraid to confront him with her." However, at about 3:00 p.m., she was admitted into the stateroom where Wendling was being held. Chief Lindsey told her that "this man has openly declared that you bear a bad reputation in Houston; that his relations with you were improper and that he at no time entertained intentions of marriage." He asked, "What have you to say about this?"

Munea shouted that Wendling was a liar and pointed at him. She continued:

> *I did not know you were so low, Jacquemin, as to try to drag a decent woman down to the level of these other women you have been going with. Although I refused to listen to your proposals of marriage, because I knew you were a thief and that there was something else wrong with you, I never dreamed that you could be so low as to want to ruin not only me, but to taint the name of my little daughter. I hate you, Jacquemin, and I hope that you will be punished for this crime if you are guilty of it.*
>
> *I have taken this long trip and subjected myself to this embarrassing position to defend my good name and protect my child. I defy you to prove these things you have said, but you can't. You said that because you thought I would never be brought before you again. You did want to marry me. You brought the ring, tried to put it on my finger, but I left the room and flatly refused to have anything to do with you. I admit once you did intrude into my room, and before I could help myself you kissed me. But you know that I went outside at once and called my aunt. I told her that I was afraid of you and she came in the next room, where she remained until you had left.*

Wendling raged at her, stating, "How can I expect any better from you, you turned me over. You did me wrong; now you want to put two charges against me. I no say these things. I only say what I heard and you know I did not harm you."

He did, however, finally admit he lied, presumably about Munea, and the unpleasant encounter ended. Interested passengers on the train hovered near the stateroom, and when the voices of those inside were raised, they were clearly audible and "furnished food for gossip" for passengers during the rest of the trip.

After resting briefly from her ordeal, Munea consented to tell her story to reporters traveling with the party. In particular, she stated:

> One of the strangest things about Wendling was a story he told me one evening as we sat on my aunt's porch in Houston. He said that while in Galveston, he had his fortune told and the clairvoyant said that he would meet a light haired man soon who would give him trouble. On the train from Galveston to Houston he accordingly fell in with a German who answered this description, and Wendling at once began to suspicion him, although they were often together in Houston. As the thing turned out, he did have reason to fear this particular man for he was the one who gave to Captain Carney the first trace of Wendling's whereabouts.

At about 6:00 p.m., the train reached St. Louis. The entire party got off. Hundreds had gathered, and photographers tried to snap photos of the group. Unlike his prior, jovial behavior with reporters, however, Wendling covered his face with his hands and tried to stay out of the way of the cameras; he also refused to talk. He was shoved into a waiting automobile provided by Chief Young and rushed to the city jail to await the final leg of his journey. There he was held in solitary confinement. The reporters noted that Captain Carney continued to suffer from extreme fatigue after his long travels; it was expected that he would take the opportunity to rest up a bit in St. Louis. Chief Lindsey, however, continued on to Louisville to prepare for Wendling's arrival, pledging that he would be protected. He reiterated that in the eyes of the law, Wendling was innocent and that he would not stand for him to be mistreated in any way.

Cora Munea was invited by Carney to continue on to Louisville with him so that the matter of her reward could be resolved. She did ride with him to the hotel where he was staying, and he was "assiduous in guarding [her] from interviewers." Ultimately, she elected to return to Kansas City, however, and then go home to Hume. Her business had been damaged from her association with Wendling; however, she anticipated that she would move to Tulsa, Oklahoma, soon. She was confident that her interests would be overseen by Captain Carney and that she would assuredly "receive something for the unpleasant experience of being mixed up in a murder case." For his part, Carney "positively declared that he will take no part of the money," as he "simply did what was my plain duty" as a police officer.

He continued:

> I am the head of the Louisville detective department and I made up my mind that if it was in human power, I was going to catch this man. I further resolved not to come back to Louisville without him. During all the long weeks that I worked and suffered hardships of every kind, I was severely criticized by those who knew nothing of the case and were simply so blinded by the partisanship that they were willing to turn the grief of these parents into political capital. However, I bear them no malice. I have my reward and I am willing to submit my case to the good people of Louisville.
>
> As for the reward, I will not touch it. I am not working for rewards and I shall see to it that it is fairly divided among those who assisted me in the capture.

Colonel John Whallen had diligently aided Carney and Lindsey, remaining up long into the night to guard the prisoner and to give Carney the opportunity for some much-needed rest. When interviewed, he stated: "I have absolutely no interest in this matter except to do all in my power to find out whether or not this man is guilty. What those fellows down there will say about it I don't care. I have offered $1,000 as part of the reward for the conviction of the child's murderer, whoever he is, and I supposed I have the right to work as hard as I can to make myself pay my own money."

Captain Carney, while out on a stroll in St. Louis, was recognized by "one of the cleverest yeggmen[11] in the country," who called to him, "Hello, Louisville, what the devil you doing here?" Carney, who had once arrested the man in Chicago, renewed his acquaintance. When he was assured that the man had retired from criminal activities, Carney bade him a cordial farewell.

While stopped over in St. Louis, Captain Carney was pulled into the investigation of the murder of another child, in 1908, in Kirkwood, Missouri. The suspect resembled Wendling by description in some respects and "had a mania for having his picture taken in the uniform of the French Army." However, Carney found little resemblance to Wendling when he actually viewed the photo. Later, Wendling's brother-in-law attested to the fact that Wendling could have had nothing to do with that crime, as he had not left Louisville for three years, until he fled in January.

Left at the jail, Wendling cried when the lights were turned down and begged that the lights be left on.

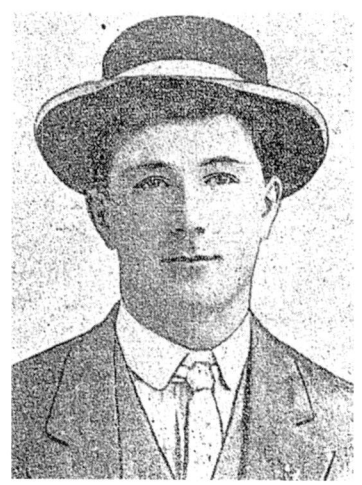

"Wendling as He Looked a Week Ago in San Francisco," published in the *Courier-Journal*.

The next day, still in St. Louis, Wendling was "put through another severe grilling" by Captain Carney. This time, at Wendling's demand, a clerk took down the interrogation. Wendling left the "sweating" "a mass of nerves." He was allowed to talk to the press and agreed to having his photo taken, but only if he was shaved. He was taken to a local barbershop by the police and given a shave and then returned to the jail for a photo session.

That same morning, Captain Carney received a telegram from J. Reginald Clements to be given to Wendling. It read as follows: "Insist on being brought to Louisville at once. Public sentiment in your favor. People on the whole believe you innocent. Have no fear of mob violence. People here sane, civilized and law-abiding."

As a token of appreciation of Carney's dogged persistence in tracking down Wendling, Mayor W.O. Head had an editorial, written by Henry Watterson of the *Courier-Journal*, along with an autograph from Watterson, framed and ready to be presented on Carney's arrival. In the same frame, a letter of appreciation written by Mayor Head was included. It read as follows:

> *Capt. John P. Carney, Chief, Louisville Detective Department, City:*
>
> *This tribute to your marvelous achievement is from the pen of the dean of the American press and the peer of editorial writers the world over. It is deserved by reason of your courage, endurance and skill in detective work. Confidence and gratitude are jewels, and they will dazzle in your official record with more radiance than diamonds. This masterful testimonial from Mr. Henry Watterson, the most distinguished citizen of Louisville, expresses the unqualified appreciation of our people. With assurance of my high personal regard and best wishes for your success, believe me, very sincerely,*
> *W.O. Head, Mayor*

With Wendling in custody, although not yet returned to Louisville, there was discussion of the disposition of the various rewards that had been offered. Richard Sweet had already begun the fight to be awarded the money offered by the City of Louisville, having made his application in June. He sent a letter to the Louisville General Council, which considered the letter on June 5 and referred it to the finance committee of the body.

His letter requesting the reward read as follows:

> *To the General Council of the city of Louisville, Gentlemen:*[12]
>
> *On December 15, 1909, your body offered a reward of $1,000 for any information leading to the recovery of Alma Kellner. On May 30, 1910, I located the body of Alma Keller in the basement of the school house at St. John's church, and so notified the police department of the city of Louisville. The Coroner's inquest conclusively substantiated my statement that Alma Keller had been found by me.*
>
> *In accordance with the terms of your reward, I have made application through my attorney to the Mayor for the payment of this reward, but to this date no payment has been made me. As the offer of this reward originated with your honorable body, I now respectfully petition you to pay me this reward of $1,000 in accordance with your offer.*
>
> *R.B. Sweet*

Yet another applicant for a part of the reward had also come forward. Joe Krimmer of San Antonio claimed that he provided the vital tip that led to Wendling's capture. Krimmer operated the Dullnig wells, where Wendling had been working in Texas. He was claiming $3,500 of the reward. He had also provided Captain Carney with a postal card from Cora Munea and suggested that he keep in touch with her, as it would be a way to pick up the trail again.

And, of course, there was discussion of the cost of the manhunt. It was estimated that Carney's expenses were approximately $100 a day, between food, transportation and lodging, and there was the cost of all the mail sent to every American consulate and every postmaster in France and Germany.

Chief Lindsey returned to Louisville but did not speak as to how soon Wendling would return. He denied, in fact, having sweated Wendling and stated that he was opposed to the "third degree" system. He also denied depriving Wendling of his dinner in Kansas City, noting that they had made plans to obtain a substantial meal at the depot restaurant, but due

CRIPPEN AND HIS TYPIST ARE SILENT

Detective Is Taking Wendling Back East

ALLEGED MURDERER AND YOUNG GIRL STILL IN JAIL AT QUEBEC

SAN FRANCISCO, August 2.—In charge of Captain of Detectives J. P. Carney, through whose efforts he was run to earth, Joseph Wendling, accused of the murder of Alma Kellner of Louisville, Ky., left today for the

QUEBEC, August 2.—Dr. Crippen and Miss Leneve, the two prisoners who have focused the eyes of the world on this old French city on the St. Lawrence, slept last night the sleep of complete exhaustion following the

The *Reno Gazette Journal*, August 2, 1910. *Courtesy of the* Reno Gazette Journal.

to the train running late, they all had to make do with sandwiches, which displeased Wendling, who expected a hot meal. He also stated that two pieces of baggage had arrived from San Francisco for Wendling and that they would be held at the police station, having been expressed home by Captain Carney. The bags had not been checked but were presumed to contain Wendling's personal effects.

And Louisville waited.

8
THE WRIT

To the consternation of the Louisville authorities, on the morning of August 10, Wendling's attorneys made a motion for a writ of habeas corpus before Judge George C. Hitchcock of St. Louis Circuit Court. His Louisville attorney, Clements, had arrived at 7:00 a.m. that morning and immediately went to the offices of Joseph G. Williams and I.A. Rollins, as he needed local attorneys to assist him in the process in Missouri. He attached a lengthy petition to the motion as to why Wendling should be immediately released. Judge Hitchcock immediately issued subpoenas for Captain John P. Carney, Colonel John H. Whallen and Colonel William Young, of the St. Louis Police Department, which were placed in the hands of Deputy Sheriff William Wraussmann to serve. At that same time, a hearing was set for August 17. The Louisville men hired Thomas Rowe Jr. to represent them and responded to the courtroom as ordered, at 2:00 p.m. A hearing was set for the same time on August 11, as Rowe argued it was unfair to put off the hearing for a week "when a deliberate attempt was being made to interfere with the wheels of justice." In response, Clements argued that Carney should set forth in full the evidence he had of Wendling's guilt.

Clements's petition was as follows:

> *In the Circuit Court, City of St. Louis, State of Missouri, City of St. Louis—To the Hon. George C. Hitchcock, Judge of the Circuit Court of the City of St. Louis:*
>
> *Affiant, J. Reginald Clements, states that he is regularly licensed and duly qualified practicing attorney of the city of Louisville, and that he*

> is the regularly employed attorney and agent of Joseph Wendling, who is unlawfully deprived of his liberty by Capt. J.P. Carney, one John H. Whallen and Capt. William Young, Chief of Police of the city of St. Louis. And is now held in the police holdover in said city; that said Wendling is held by the aforesaid parties and confined in the police holdover without warrant, order or process of law and without any authority. That said petitioner is held under a supposed indictment for a supposed crime for murder, which is alleged to have been committed in the county of Jefferson, State of Kentucky, on the – day of –, 1909, and that there is no warrant, commitment or order of any court under which said petitioner is held.
>
> Your petitioner further states that said imprisonment is illegal in this, to-wit; That crime he is held and confined for in said prison is one that was committed in the State of Kentucky and that none of said parties that are holding him has any warrant, commitment, order of court or requisition papers to take this said petitioner out of the State of Missouri back to the State of Kentucky, where said crime was supposed to have been committed and where they are intending to take your petitioner.
>
> Your petitioner further states that the aforesaid parties are about to and intend to unlawfully take said prisoner out of the State of Missouri and into the State of Kentucky.
>
> Your petitioner further states that no application for the relief sought has been made to or refused by any court, officer or officers, superior to the one to whom this petition is presented.
>
> Your petitioner further represents that he is unlawfully deprived of his liberty.
>
> Wherefore, your petitioner prays that the writ of habeas corpus may be issued, that he may be discharged from said holdover and said unlawful imprisonment.
>
> This affiant, J. Reginald Clements, the attorney and agent of Joseph Wendling for him and his behalf, makes oath and says that the facts stated in the above petition are true and correct according to his best knowledge and belief.

Clements signed the document, and it was notarized by Isaac Rollins.

The response filed by Howe, on the part of the three men, was simply: "The defendants state under oath that they make a denial in toto of every charge in the plaintiff's petition contained."

Clements, being interviewed by the media, claimed: "As our petition shows, the poor, unfortunate man is being deprived of his liberty. By deceit, treachery, harassing, intimidation and the most shameful of treatment men are trying to put the blame for that crime on the head of an innocent man. All the way across the country they have been mistreating him and we don't propose to stand for it any longer. There is no question but that this court has jurisdiction on this matter and we will succeed in getting our man away from these men."

Dr. Hill, however, contacted over the long-distance telephone, "said that nothing could be further from the truth." He asked that the following statement be published:

> *I never in all my life saw a man accused for such a grave crime and on such good grounds treated with as much kindness as was Joseph Wendling. I was on the train when he was being brought from Kansas City to St. Louis, and as a student of psychology asked that I might speak to him for just a moment. My request was granted and I went into the stateroom where Wendling was in the custody of Chief Lindsey. After being in there for a reasonable length of time I suppose I should have withdrawn when it was announced that he was to be questioned again, but again on my request I was permitted to remain.*
>
> *I remember distinctly of Colonel Lindsey saying: "Doctor, there is no reason why you should not hear all that goes on here. I have resolved that no unfair advantage be taken of this man. We are simply trying to question him and get the truth from him. We do not care where this leads us; we want to see the guilty man punished."*
>
> *The "sweating" of Wendling was carried on in a most kindly manner. He was repeatedly told that everything that he said was to be used as evidence against him and no unfair advantages were ever taken of him. On the contrary, to his being in the gang of men who would mistreat him the Louisville party is composed of as gentlemanly, intelligent and human officers as I have ever seen.*

Attorney Rowe focused on the validity of the papers being carried by Captain Carney to justify the arrest and transportation of Wendling back to Louisville. When taken into custody and arraigned in California, Wendling had agreed to return to Louisville without further paperwork needed. Carney had in his possession requisition orders, if needed, from both the governor of Texas and the governor of California and was acting as Governor Willson's agent in returning Wendling to Kentucky "and has the right to bring his prisoner through any State in the Union." Only the U.S. District Court had any jurisdiction in the matter, and Rowe stated that Captain Carney was willing to submit his case to any judge.

Carney telegraphed the following to Chief Lindsey: "Tied up here with habeas corpus proceedings. Everything all right. Hearing 2 o'clock tomorrow and their move will fail. See through the whole affair."

He later described the effort to a newspaper reporter: "This is simply a political move on the part of those who have been bantering us to capture Wendling to see him free after we have succeeded in running him down. They will leave no stone unturned to turn this affair into votes. If Wendling is not guilty no one would rather see him go scot free than I, but I do not propose to allow these persons to interfere with justice. I shall carry this matter to the highest court in the land if necessary and show these fellows a thing or two."

The reporters even went to the former governor of Missouri, Charles P. Johnson, for an opinion on the chances of the case. He was given a chance to examine the papers submitted to the court and stated:

> *Under the law there is no way for a Missouri court to set free this man. He is not only wanted charged with a most heinous crime, but he is indicted on that charge, a bench warrant is in the possession of the man who has him in charge and the only court in the world which has any jurisdiction in the matter is the Circuit Court of Jefferson County.*
>
> *Of course, it is only right that any citizen should have the privilege to appeal for a writ of habeas corpus from any court in the land, but that court can only decide on the point as to whether he is being illegally held. If this Louisville officer has a bench warrant issued on an indictment then there is nothing for Judge Hitchcock to do but to deny this writ. Under the law Wendling is not being illegally held as long as he is held under due process of the law. Of course, he has the right to contest extradition from California, but as he has waived this right, then there are absolutely no merits in that petition drawn up by his attorney.*
>
> *Even though he did not waive extradition and now wishes to contest his removal to Kentucky and Judge Hitchcock dismisses him from custody that will not prevent his being held. All that Capt. Carney or anyone who can swear that Wendling is wanted in Kentucky on a murder charge, will have to do is to swear out a warrant charging him with the crime. Then he can be rearrested and held awaiting requisition papers on the Governor of Missouri. The matter could also be carried to the United States Court and an injunction could be obtained against Judge Hitchcock preventing him*

from granting the habeas corpus writ. However, I believe that there will be little to the affair and that Judge Hitchcock will find nothing else to do but to dismiss the petition of these lawyers.

After Carney received the subpoena, he was asked by Clements and his Missouri colleagues to be allowed to speak to the prisoner. Captain Carney agreed to that being done at 4:00 p.m., on the condition that he remain with Wendling during the interview. Clements, however, hurried to the judge and asked that they be allowed to speak to Wendling and received an order allowing him to do so. He then went to Chief Young with that order. Young admitted them at once, and Clements engaged in a long discussion with his client, cautioning him "against making any damaging statements or above all a confession of any kind." Carney was indignant about the process. Clements, in the meantime, had wired Frankfort and requested Governor Willson send someone else to transport Wendling back to Kentucky, if that became necessary. He requested, specifically, the sheriff of Jefferson County to take charge of the prisoner.

In the meantime, Captain Carney "induced Assistant Circuit Attorney Davis to issue an information charging Wendling with being a fugitive from justice" in Kentucky. It was sworn to before Judge Benjamin Klene and would be used only if Judge Hitchcock ruled against the Louisville officers.

On August 11, 1910, Hitchcock convened the hearing at the appointed hour. Wendling was brought in by the St. Louis authorities holding him, Chief of Detectives James Smith and Detectives Murphy and Quinn. Attorney Rowe moved to have Chief of Police William Young and Colonel John H. Whallen dismissed, as they had no authority in the holding of Wendling. This was granted immediately. Captain Carney then presented his case, setting out the facts and citing the warrant he held from Kentucky. During an impassioned plea to the court, Wendling's attorneys argued for his release, to which Rowe simply responded that "there was no question involved except the validity of the papers on which the prisoner was being held and that he would not go into any other point."

Clements shouted that he should "show us the papers then. We're in Missouri now and no statements go." Rowe "drew from his pocket a package of gold-sealed and ribbon-bedecked documents that caused a panic among the opposition lawyers." In the bundle Rowe proffered to the court was a "copy of the indictment against Wendling, a bench warrant for his return to Louisville, requisition papers on the Governor of Texas and on the governor of California and an appointment of Capt. Carney as the agent of Gov.

Willson." Judge Hitchcock refused a request from the defense attorneys for time to study the documents and admitted all of the documents except those directed to Texas as evidence. (Those documents were ruled irrelevant to the case at hand.)

Wendling was placed on the stand and identified himself as Henri Joseph Wendling. He was led by his attorney into stating that he "no want to go back," at least, not with Carney. After a brief questioning by Rowe, the judge concluded that "there was no point at question except the validity of Capt. Carney's papers." Clements continued to argue that his client was being mistreated and was ordered by the judge to "produce your proof of intimidation being tolerated in the jurisdiction of this court and it may have some bearing on the outcome of this case." However, Clements was unable to do so. The judge noted that they seemed to be arguing to turn Wendling loose in Missouri, rather than getting him back to Kentucky. Clements finally agreed to dismiss the motion, provided he could accompany Wendling. The judge noted it could not enter into such an agreement and turned Wendling over to Carney to be returned to Kentucky.

In an exciting departure, once Carney was given permission to leave St. Louis, the officers hustled Wendling over the bridge crossing the Mississippi River to East St. Louis, in Illinois, to avoid any further efforts in Missouri to free him. Wendling "seemed to enjoy the fun of dodging the many machines that were following the Louisville party" in their dash from Missouri. He was to wait in East St. Louis in jail until the Louisville train was scheduled to leave St. Louis. Clements followed them to East St. Louis and appealed to Judge George A. Crow of St. Clair County, Illinois, to issue a writ of habeas corpus. The judge agreed, but only if Wendling was still in his jail at noon the next day. Learning of this from the local police chief, Carney went to the jail in a taxi, which he left waiting a block away, and walked to the station. He demanded his prisoner from Night Chief Overmeyer. Wendling was awakened. Carrying his collar in one hand and coat and hat in the other, he "refused to budge" until given time to "spruce up" a bit. He was assisted in attaching his collar, brushing his hair and dusting off his shoes. Carney "hurried Wendling westward across the bridge, in a taxicab, at midnight." They left on the Baltimore & Ohio Southwestern at 1:45 a.m. for an unknown destination. Carney stated to reporters, "I am forced to act like a fugitive myself in order to escape this effort to hinder justice."

At the St. Louis Union Station train depot, Patrolman Chase, seeing the party hurrying away, telephoned Chief William Young to determine if he about midnight and taken to the police station to await the train. Once boarded, they bedded down for the trip, with Carney and Wendling still shackled together. Wendling was restless and finally woke for good at 5:00 a.m., so they moved into the stateroom, where Wendling chewed on a cigar. He expressed confidence, however, that his attorney would get him out of the charges.

The newspaper reported: "Unless all plans miscarry Captain Carney will have landed his prisoner in Louisville before 8 o'clock to-morrow morning, after the longest and probably the greatest chase in detective history."

9
THE ARRIVAL

At long last, on August 12, Joseph Wendling arrived in Louisville. His attorney had preceded him, having continued on the same train from which Carney had removed Wendling. When Clements arrived, he immediately went to his South Floyd street home "to get some much needed rest."

As the train entered Louisville, Wendling saw with pleasure that curious eyes turned upon him. He waved delightedly at those who watched the train as it lumbered into the city. He arrived at the Tenth street train station at 8:15 a.m., by way of the Henderson route. He walked out with his wrists handcuffed together. He was met by Chief Lindsey and a larger, curious crowd and hurried to a waiting police car, still shackled to Captain Carney. As soon as he was inside, the driver took the vehicle at top speed east on Broadway, then north on Seventh street to Jefferson street, and then up Jefferson to city hall at Sixth street.[13] Another large crowd awaited them there. Wendling was rushed into Lindsey's office and was met by Joseph M. Huffaker, the commonwealth attorney. There, the bloody clothing found in his room was shown to Wendling, and he admitted that the items belonged to him. He did not acknowledge ownership of the green hat, with its three bloody fingerprints, however. Just as they were showing him the bloody trousers, Clements caught up with them and told Wendling to answer no more questions. Wendling was then taken to the jail, just a block away, to be slated by Chief Deputy Jailer Eugene Blanford.

Deputy Blanford asked, "What is the charge, Captain?" to which Carney replied, "He has already been indicted. Charge him with murder." Wendling was searched and had in his possession only sixty cents, left from the five dollars he had when he left California. The inmates in the jail were just as interested as everyone else to see the new prisoner, so Jailer John R. Pflanz paraded him around the tiers so that everyone could view him, a process Wendling enjoyed very much. He was then placed in seclusion, with only police officials and Clements allowed to see him. Once Carney placed his prisoner into the custody of the jailer, he immediately left for his home, at 1301 Washington street (now East Washington street), presumably to be greeted by his wife, Mary, and two sons, Edward and John P., as well as his aged mother, Johana. It was later reported that after some much-needed rest, he began to look through his mail, finding in the batch of letters awaiting him "words of congratulation from chiefs of police in practically every large city in the United States, from detective agencies and private citizens." Most prized, however, was a letter from W.A. Pinkerton, the head of the Pinkerton National Detective Agency, which read as follows:

Pinkerton National Detective Agency, Chicago, Ill., 204 Fifth Avenue.—Saratoga Springs, N.Y., Aug. 4, 1910.: Captain John P. Carney, Esq.; Chief of Detectives, Louisville, Ky.—

My Dear Chief:
I wish to tender you my heartiest congratulations in running down Wendling. I consider that it was one of the greatest pieces of detective work I have ever known in years, and I am glad of the fact that you are indebted to nothing but your own ability and skill in tracing this clever fugitive to his lair and effecting his capture.

I have watched the papers with deep interest, not only on account of the brutality of the crime, but on account of the skill you displayed in following up Wendling. None of your friends wish you more hearty congratulations than I do. The successful termination of this hard-won, splendid achievement is one that any detective in the world might be proud of.

I arrived here on Monday night in connection with the race meeting, and I will remain during the month of August. My address is, Congress Hall Hotel in this city, and I will be pleased to have a line from you when you get time to write. If I had known you were going to California I would have tendered you the services of our offices at San Francisco and Los Angeles, but I knew nothing of your route. I know you met with the most

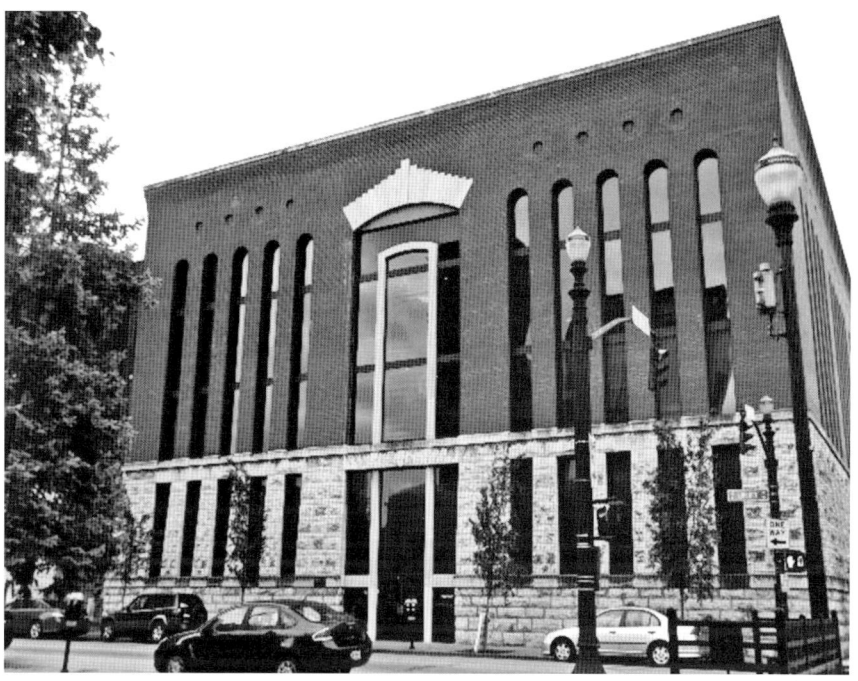

Jefferson County Jail. *Courtesy of Louisville Metro Archives.*

cordial reception from the police in San Francisco, as John Martin is a big fellow like yourself in mannerisms, and is one of the finest men in the world. Starting out on such a trail without much of a clew you certainly are entitled to be congratulated on your success.

With kindest personal regards, I am, sincerely yours,
W.A. Pinkerton

In addition to the letters of commendation, he received a number of job offers and at least one letter requesting his help in finding a missing grandchild. For the rest of the day, Captain Carney was kept busy with telephone calls from friends. On his arrival earlier, he had been met at city hall by a "crowd of enthusiastic friends" who had nearly worn out his arm from shaking. He received a slap on the back from Mayor Head. The mayor stated: "Well, John, I am proud of you and the people of Louisville are proud of you, and we are glad that you are back among us, as we missed you while you were away working so hard and fearlessly to capture this man."

At his return, it was noted, Carney was planning to take a well-deserved vacation in the country with his family. Colonel John Whallen was also "almost completely worn out by his long journey."

Wendling was provided with a special breakfast on his arrival but was to receive only regular jail fare from that point forward and was to be treated the same as other prisoners. It was anticipated that his case would be called in the October term of the circuit court. Clements was given the opportunity to talk to his client immediately, and they spoke at length. He left and returned with Lena Wendling but was told that she would not be permitted to see her husband. Clements tried to get a court order to allow her to see the prisoner but was unsuccessful. Clements returned to the jail and took her and a relative, John Kippes, to his office instead.[14] He returned later with a change of linen for Wendling, presumably a clean shirt and underwear. Lena was described as ill the next day, when reporters called on her brother's home at 1528 Southgate.

Chief Ellis of Houston, it was reported, was seeking a part of the reward. He arrived on August 15 and met with Louisville police authorities the next day. He engaged an attorney to represent his interests, William Marshall Bullitt, and was asking for one-half of the available reward money. He felt the remainder should be given to Cora Munea and the two detectives who actually captured Wendling in San Francisco. He objected to the suggestion that he was entitled to only $1,000, at most. After spending the night at the Seelbach Hotel, he returned to Houston. At the same time, a letter arrived from Edward Artz, the foreman at the place where Wendling had worked, also seeking a share of the reward. Chief Lindsey noted that they had to concentrate first on convicting Wendling, then the matter of the reward would be taken up.

On August 13, Jailer John R. Pflanz agreed to allow Lena Wendling in to see her husband, but she did not make a request to do so. She did drop off a basket of fruit for him, however. Attorney Clements had moved the court to order the jailer to allow no one in to see Wendling without giving notice to Clements. Judge Gregory, however, denied that motion.

Joseph Wendling made a public appeal:

> *To the Public: I am innocent of the charges made against me. My wife and I are without adequate means to defray the expenses of my defense. I am a foreigner in your country. There are powerful interests allied against me. I do not ask for mercy, but I appeal to every person in this community who has regard for justice to contribute such financial assistance as they can afford,*

in order to insure me a fair and lawful trial. Secure in my own knowledge of my innocence, I ask only a fair and lawful trial, and I cannot have my case fairly tried without money to pay lawyers and expenses. I feel that there is fairness enough in this community to help me to this and to see the guilty person punished, whoever he may be.

Send money in care of our attorney, J. Reginald Clements, 503-4-5 Kentucky Title building, who will make accounting and see the money is properly expended. We will publish names of those who desire, and only at their request. Those who do not care to disclose their names need not do so.

It was signed Joseph and Lena Wendling.

Mr. Fehr, in the meantime, expressed his thanks to Colonel John H. Whallen.

Marine Hotel, Highland Park, Chicago, Ill., Aug. 12, 1910.—Col. John H. Whallen, Louisvilley, Ky.:

My Dear Colonel:
On behalf of myself and the other members of the Kellner family, I take this means of now thanking you and your brother, and expressing to you both our warm appreciation of your untiring efforts and active assistance rendered in the furtherance of the cause of justice in this community.

Your wise counsel and wide experience gained while Chief of Police of this city, were not only invaluable, but were always at our service from the time this terrible sorrow first came upon us down to the present time.

Last winter when we were in doubt as to just the best method to pursue, and first went to you and sought your advice and assistance, you and your brother promptly and freely gave it: and further offered a reward of $500 for the return of the missing child, and then in May last increased it to $1,000 for the capture and conviction of the murderer.

Throughout these long and tiring months to us, when we have time and time again asked your help, neither you nor your brother have ever hesitated for a moment, but both of you have done everything in your power to comply with our requests, even though at times at personal inconvenience, expense and sacrifice to yourselves.

When things have looked discouraging you never lost heart of a moment, but effectively assisted us and the officers of the law in keeping up the search for the guilty party, no matter where the trail might lead, and until the capture and safe return to Louisville of the fugitive now under indictment by the grand jury.

And realizing that you have but recently recovered from a severe illness, we appreciate all the more your efforts and ready compliance with everything asked of you.

Your valuable assistance to the officers of the law having been rendered from beginning to end solely at the request of myself and the Kellner family, we beg to assure you that the same, as well as your friends show to us at this time, will always be remembered. I am, sincerely your friend.
Frank Fehr

And finally, on August 13, 1910, Captain John P. Carney, the Louisville chief of detectives, was back at his desk, before any of his detectives had arrived. He and his secretary, Edward Mackey, kept busy all day going through the "vast heap of mail" that had accumulated, sorting the regular business of the office from the numerous notes of congratulations. Like those he received at home, some requested help as well, including one from an aged spinster whose long-lost sweetheart had left her, saying he was going to get a marriage license and never returned. As with all such letters, his response would be that, since he was connected to the police department, he could not engage in any private detective work.

On August 15, 1910, Lena Wendling finally met her husband again, in a most affectionate manner, but under the watchful eye of a guard. She hugged and kissed him, and Joseph, in turn, seemed very happy to see her. She left him one dollar to purchase "little things that would bring him comfort" while jailed. They shook hands on her departure.

10

THE PRETRIAL

With Joseph Wendling finally in custody, the legal proceedings could move forward.

As he sat in the Jefferson County Jail, Wendling remained cheerful. He enjoyed his jail fare, along with the delicacies allowed for a Sunday meal, and made friends with other prisoners on his tier once he was allowed to interact with them. They wiled away the day playing checkers, a game that was new and a mystery to him. He was kept under constant watch by several trusty prisoners who were friendly but were placed there to "watch his every move and prevent the possibility of any outbreak." In the mornings, they would file a report with the jailers on how Wendling slept, what he was doing and his overall physical and mental condition. Guards were to always be present during any visits, as well.

New witnesses were beginning to be identified in the local newspaper. Two local physicians, Dr. J.C. Morrison and Dr. John J. Connelley, came forward, stating that they had been called upon to dress the wound Wendling sustained the year before, which he claimed was the source of the bloodstained clothing. The doctors declared that the injury occurred in January 1909 and that Wendling was found with a bullet in his hand, which had to be extracted, in great pain and with profuse bleeding. Both agreed that they had been told that the wound was caused by an accidental discharge from a pistol.

In an effort to raise funds, on September 5, 1910, Lena Wendling visited Phoenix Hill Park during a Labor Day celebration and attempted to sell photographs of her husband. The committee in charge of the event agreed that it was "not the proper time nor place" to do so, telling her that she could not sell the photos inside the park. She readily assented and left.

The Louisville General Council was presented with a voucher of $432 for the expenses of Captain Carney for his trip to San Francisco and back. When added to the expense report already submitted, the entire amount expended on the manhunt came to about $1,000, considerably less than previously reported.

Even though Wendling was in custody, there were still individuals being watched and arrested if they were believed to be Wendling. As late as September 10, it was reported, a possible suspect had been identified and was being watched in Japan, as was communicated in a letter to Chief Lindsey. He cabled the authorities there that, although Wendling was in custody, he appreciated the actions of the Japanese authorities and their efforts to help. He noted that it showed that the bulletins did go out across the world and that "everybody was on the lookout."

J. Reginald Clements, it was noted, was receiving numerous threatening letters demanding he quit the case and leave Louisville. He stated that he refused to be "bluffed."

The annual report of the police department was filed with the Board of Public Safety on September 22, 1910. It gave the complement of the department as 413 men, with 58 officers, 1 chief of detectives, 1 secretary for the department and the detectives' department, 10 detectives, 1 stenographer, 1 messenger, 12 district detectives, 1 property clerk, 1 printer, 1 police court officer, 6 chauffeurs, 2 auto guards, 26 station keepers and 23 wagon guards; this left 268 men as patrolmen. (The numbers do not add up to 413; the math in the report was inaccurate.)

Of course, the Wendling case was mentioned. Chief Lindsey stated: "I wish to respectfully call attention to the efficient and untiring service rendered by Capt. J.P. Carney, chief of detectives, in his overland chase which resulted in the final capture of Joseph Wendling, the alleged murderer of Alma Kellner."

At long last, on October 3, 1910, Joseph Wendling's name appeared at the top of the docket in the Jefferson Criminal Court for his arraignment. A crowd gathered, although not as many as might be expected given the high profile of the case. He was held in the prisoner room in the back of the main courtroom until 11:30 a.m., and many spectators left before he was brought before the judge. When asked to enter a plea, he replied, "I'm not guilty." At the arraignment, Wendling demanded that he was entitled to be tried by a jury made up of six aliens and six citizens, an "ancient mode of trial by jury." Although the right was embodied in Kentucky state law, there was no mechanism in state law to summon such a jury, since Kentucky law also required that all jurors be citizens. As such, he demanded his case be removed to federal court, where such jurors could be called.

Wendling also submitted an affidavit claiming that when the grand jury had initially concluded, there was insufficient cause to return an indictment and that Chief Lindsey became personally involved and importuned them to return an indictment, and eventually, they did so.

A hearing on the motion was scheduled, and Wendling was passed back out of the courtroom and returned to the jail via a tunnel. When the new jail was constructed a few years before, it was several blocks farther from the court buildings than the previous jail had been. The county found itself with the need to transport prisoners safely in some way back and forth from court. The problem was solved with the construction of a tunnel that led from the basement of the jail,[15] northward under Green and Jefferson streets, the Jefferson County Courthouse and Court Alley, and into the basement of the building directly to the north of the rear of the courthouse, then used for the criminal courts. That tunnel remained in use until the construction of the next jail, in the mid-1970s.

At the subsequent hearing, on October 19, Judge Walter Evans of the U.S. District Court heard the arguments from both sides on the removing

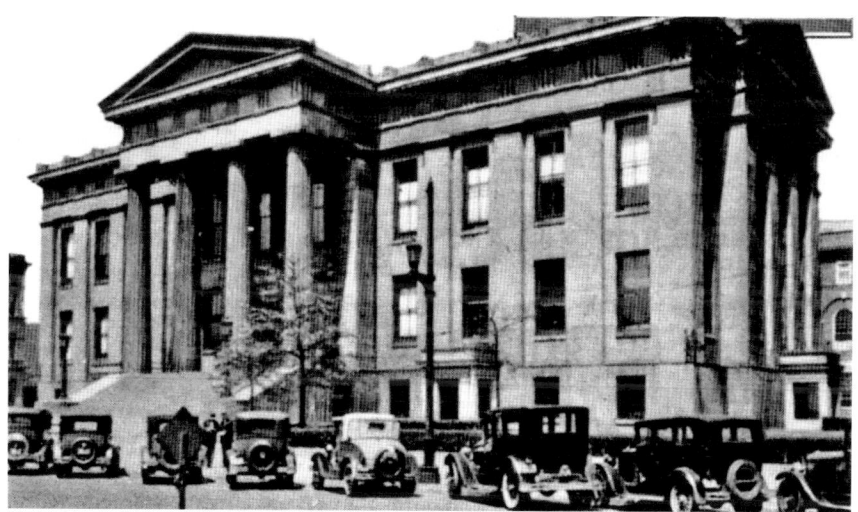

Jefferson County Courthouse, Louisville, Kentucky. *www.Kaintuckeean.com*.

of the case to the federal court located at the customhouse. Attorney John Ray represented Wendling, while assistant commonwealth's attorney Loraine Mix opposed the motion. Ray argued that, although the law came into existence during the reign of Edward IV, it had never been repealed. Wendling, an unnaturalized alien, was entitled to trial under that law. After questioning Ray at length, Judge Evans announced that he did not need to hear from the commonwealth.

The next morning, Judge Evans summarily denied the petition to transfer the case and agreed that the matter should stay within the jurisdiction of the Kentucky courts. In his opinion on the issue of the statute, he agreed that the "two sections of the Kentucky statutes cited by the attorneys for Wendling must be construed together and that if there is any conflict between the two sections doubtless the State Courts will endeavor so to construe them as to harmonize them and give effect to both." He suggested that there was no indication that as an alien, Wendling was not being accorded the equal protection of the law, and that jurors serving in the U.S. District Court must have the same qualifications as those in Kentucky—in other words, the federal courts could not seat aliens, either.

Section 2253 of the Kentucky Statutes stated: "No person shall be a competent juryman for the trial of criminal, penal or civil cases in any court unless he be a citizen, at least 21 years of age, a housekeeper, sober, temperate, discreet and of good demeanor." But in a hangover from old law, the very next statute, Section 2254, stated that "Juries de medietate linguae may be directed by the court." The court agreed that such a jury (six aliens and six citizens of Kentucky) "would seem to depend upon the discretion of the court." The court noted that, in fact, Wendling had not even as yet actually asked for such a jury but was basing his argument on the fact that, apparently, Kentucky could not have such a jury. Since the Kentucky courts had not yet had an opportunity to deny him the right provided in the statute, the federal courts could not intervene. Judge Evans remanded the case back to the criminal division of the Jefferson Circuit Court.

The march toward trying Joseph Wendling moved apace. On November 14, 1910, an order was entered indicating that Sergeant Thomas Burke of the San Francisco Police Department and Mrs. Cora Munea of Hume, Missouri, were necessary witnesses to Wendling's trial, scheduled for November 28. As such, their expenses would be paid by the State of Kentucky for their appearance.

The next day, Clements moved that Dr. Duncan be ordered to turn over the evidence presented in the coroner's inquest to the clerk of the court so that Clements might be able to examine it. Further, he demanded a copy of the evidence, in effect, the transcript of the coroner's inquest, which was in the possession of the commonwealth's attorney. But Clarence Walker, the stenographer, did not wish to produce another copy unless he was paid for it. (He had initially been paid $150 for his services.) Mix argued that "it was a matter of choice with the Fiscal Court to pay for the transcript, and it was for the benefit of the Commonwealth." At the hearing on November 16, Judge Gregory ruled that the coroner "must either turn over to the Criminal Court Clerk the substance in writing of the evidence or the entire transcript of the testimony taken at the inquest" on or before November 18. In fact, Ray argued that state law required the coroner to have turned the transcript itself over to the court so that all parties could have access to it but that, instead, Duncan had given it to the commonwealth's attorney.

Judge Gregory ruled that "he did not think the Fiscal Court had a right under the statute to pay for the transcript out of the public funds, as the law provides how the Coroner shall have such work done." Since it was, in fact, already done, that was a moot point, however. The following day, Mix announced in court that he was ready to file the document, and he did so.

On November 19, Detective Burke set out eastward for Louisville on the train from California.

On November 21, Judge Gregory overruled the motion for a jury de mediate linguae made by Wendling's attorney. He had thoroughly reviewed the history of the statute and noted that the only case he could find in which the process was used was in Virginia in 1828. The judge agreed that the Constitution preserved the right of a trial by jury, rather than a particular mode or means of a jury trial. It distinguished the trial by a judge alone, or "any of the other ancient methods of trial, as by ordeal, wage of battle, etc." He also overruled a motion that all articles of clothing exhibited to the coroner's jury and the grand jury be placed with the clerk of the court. Captain Carney had agreed that the attorneys could view the evidence, presumably at the police station. The judge agreed that that was sufficient and, further, that it was unnecessary for Wendling to go along, as his attorneys had requested, as he'd already seen the items and as "the jail is the place for him." Wendling was brought into the court to hear the judge's rulings.

By November 26, 1910, Munea and Burke had arrived in Louisville. Munea immediately called Carney on her arrival but refused to speak to reporters, stating that publicity had already ruined her business and she would be relocating from Hume soon. Burke also visited Carney and then went to the Louisville Hotel to rest, as he was greatly fatigued from his long trip. It was expected that he and Carney would take a tour of the city the next day, a Sunday. Captain Carney and Dr. Robins were busy, in the meantime, getting the evidence ready for the presentation.

As was becoming the norm for reporters covering the fashionable Cora Munea, the newspaper reported her attire in careful detail. Upon her arrival in Louisville, it was noted, she "wore a tailored suit of light brown, made with the popular semi-hobble style of skirt, and short coat. Her hat was of petunia velvet with a willow plume."

11

The Trial

On Monday, November 28, 1910, the first day of the trial, Joseph Wendling once again gained front-page status in the *Courier-Journal*. It was noted that "some of the most interesting scientific evidence ever heard in a local courtroom will be introduced" on the issue of the actual identity of the charred bones.

The newspaper speculated that morning that several hundred people would be crowded into the criminal courtroom and that many more would be turned away. Since Wendling would be brought through the tunnel from the jail, those outside the immediate area of the courtroom would not have the chance to see him. It was assumed that it would take some time to select a jury, however, so no excitement could be expected for several days at least.

Before Wendling was brought over through the tunnel by Deputy Jailer John W. Moeller, he had already been busy. The prisoner was awakened at about 5:00 a.m. to perform his usual morning duties at the jail as "cage boss." In that position, he enjoyed his role of being in charge of feeding his fellow prisoners. When visited by the newspapermen on Sunday, it was observed that he had gained a great deal of weight. He remained confident that he would be acquitted and expressed his willingness to help find who actually did commit the murder. Wendling extolled the virtues of his long-suffering wife, Lena, who brought him clean clothes and nice things to eat and who was working to set him free. Following his morning tasks, Wendling prepared for his appearance. It was noted that he seemed more concerned with how he was dressed than about the trial itself. He was assisted in his grooming by

Toyo Yosnida, a Japanese man accused of the theft of a diamond stickpin who was "able to add many skillful touches to the Frenchman's makeup."

On November 28, 1910, at 10:30 a.m., the Jefferson Circuit Court, Criminal Division, with Judge James P. Gregory on the bench, convened. Wendling was brought from the prisoners' room, where he had been smoking a cigar. As expected, the courtroom was "crowded to the doors with men, women and children, anxious to catch sight of the prisoner." Wendling was attired in the same dove-gray suit he'd worn on his trip from San Francisco, with a "knit silk four-in-hand tie." He had been freshly shaved and his hair was trimmed; he wore a tan telescope hat with a broad brim. He passed through the crowd, recognizing friends and speaking to them. He also greeted Captain Carney and inquired about his well-being, to which the police officer stated he was "never in better health." Wendling took his seat between his attorneys briefly but was returned to the prisoners' room while Judge Gregory disposed of several minor cases. He finally called for Wendling's case, and Wendling was brought back into the courtroom.

Entering behind Wendling was Michael Hermann, a wine merchant and French consul, and they chatted in French. When asked by newspaper reporters, he noted that as a representative of the French government, it was his duty to assist a fellow countryman. He had employed Wendling at one time and had come to his aid as an advisor and interpreter. Lena Wendling greeted her husband with a handshake, inquiring about how he'd slept. She wore a "neat black suit, wore a dark striped raincoat and a small black hat, trimmed in black satin ribbon."

By that time, the "crowd in the courtroom had become so large and so noisy that Judge Gregory ordered the Deputy Sheriffs and the police under Lieutenant McElliott, to clear the passageways for witnesses and court officers, and the inside space, reserved for those connected with the case." The judge cautioned the spectators that he would tolerate no disturbances. Both sides announced that they were ready for trial. The lists of prosecution and defense witnesses were published, and the witnesses were sworn in. One witness, however, was not present, Dr. J.C. Morrison, for the defense. Judge Gregory issued an attachment for him, to ensure he would be available when needed.

When the names of the potential jury members were called, many crowded around the bench, seeking to be excused. The judge held firm, however, noting, "It is the duty of every good citizen to serve when called upon, else the greatest institution of our civilization will come into disrepute.

You are called for jury service no oftener than once a year, and unless you have very good reasons you must serve."

He did excuse some due to old age, illness and "being registered pharmacists or because of pressing business engagements." After the first panel was seated, Joseph Huffaker put a series of questions to them, much like those put to jurors today. He excluded four, and others took their place. The defense attorneys had their turn, and they excluded all but five. When one potential juror, a Mr. Erickson, a blacksmith, was challenged by Clements concerning his ability to hear, Erickson agreed that his hearing was bad in one ear but said that if he was seated in the first chair in the jury box, he would be able to hear the witnesses. Ultimately, however, he was not selected for the jury—Clements exercised one of his peremptory challenges to exclude him.

The crowd in the courtroom had grown, and the police officers called in to assist were hard-pressed to keep them under control. Judge Gregory had ordered that "the decorum of the courtroom must not be disturbed and the slightest noise or frivolity was 'nipped in the bud.'"

The court settled down into the business of the day. The prosecutors were seated behind a long table that faced the judge's bench. Captain Carney sat with them and was the subject of a motion to have him excluded, since he would be an important witness. Judge Gregory denied the motion, noting that "each side is entitled to have one witness remain in court." In an arrangement that would appear odd today, the defense occupied the space between the judge's bench and the table used by the commonwealth's attorneys. They had six chairs, in three rows, with Clements and Ray in front. Behind them sat Lena Wendling and Attorney Bailey. In the last row were Joseph Wendling and Michael Hermann. Like Carney, Hermann was a witness but was allowed to stay in the courtroom during the trial. Everyone else who would be a witness was banished to the witness room.

The court immediately set about the business of seating a jury, and by 2:00 p.m., five men were selected. They were, as follows: James Callahan, a grain dealer and flour manufacturer who lived on West Oak street; Ben Cohen, a merchant tailor, of South Seventh street; Peter Rohn, an expressman, of East Burnett avenue; Clement J. Brumleve, a grocer, of West Madison street; and Anton Steens, a stone engraver, of East Caldwell street.

With both the regular and the special jury panel exhausted, Judge Gregory ordered a special venire of thirty-six more men be drawn from the jury wheel. Those pulled were to report the next day. He instructed those already selected to "remain together until the trial is completed." They were them concerning the case." Should someone do so, he noted, that individual would be guilty of a serious offense. He placed the jury in the charge of Deputy Sheriffs Dennis Heffernan and Joseph Bouteiller, who escorted them to the nearby Louisville Hotel for the night. The witnesses were discharged but cautioned that they were expected to be on hand promptly every morning and to remain in the witness room unless excused. He noted that if "any witness does not abide by the instructions at this trial it will not be well for him." He then adjourned for the day.

The next day, Wednesday, was taken up with more than a dozen witnesses. From 9:00 a.m. until adjournment, a "crowd of several thousand persons jammed the courtroom and listened eagerly to the testimony." In many ways, however, much of the testimony was anticlimactic, having already been addressed in detail during the coroner's inquest.

The first witness before the jury was Fred Kellner. He identified himself as Alma's father and stated that his daughter had turned eight on October 4, 1909. He testified that he had given her breakfast on the morning of December 8, as her mother and aunt had gone to Mass. He agreed that he'd not seen her since that date and that he had diligently searched for her. Under cross-examination, he confirmed that he'd not seen the remains found at the church nor had he gone to the funeral.

Elizabeth Weitzel, Alma's aunt, was next. She testified briefly about assisting Alma to dress for church and provided a detailed description of her clothing that morning, describing her "little shepherd plaid black and white checks with velvet collar, and an emblem on the arms of the coat." The mushroom hat, made of felt with a drooped brim, was dark maroon. She was called upon to identify a stocking found with the remains and agreed it seemed identical to the one Alma would have been wearing, as was a tan gauntlet glove with a red star. Alma had worn her older, black, kid, buttoned shoes that morning, and her aunt identified the shoe displayed to her as looking very much like the shoe she had worn. Her aunt had placed in Alma's pocket a brand-new handkerchief with a crossbar in the fabric and a small bowknot in the corner. That was, she claimed, the only handkerchief Alma possessed. She agreed that Alma had several filled teeth, done by Dr. Ruby over a period of time. She also would have known how to get to St. John's Church, having gone there just the Sunday before and having gone there "right often"—although the family usually attended St. Boniface's, a few blocks farther north.

Weitzel testified that the search for Alma began in earnest between 3:00 and 3:30 p.m., when her mother "commenced to feel uneasy." Mrs. Kellner began to telephone people she knew and, when Alma was not located, set out to search.

Under cross-examination, Weitzel agreed that she had not watched Alma go down Broadway. She confirmed that she swore that the glove was Alma's glove and not one that just looked like it, as she'd handled it often. She acknowledged that the child's name was not on it, nor any other identifying mark. She did not know the size of the glove or where the pair had been purchased, either. She did not go into the details about the stocking. She agreed that she didn't know for sure, of course, that Alma had gone to St. John's the Sunday before, but only that she'd sent her there, and that she had never gone with her niece to Mass there. She had returned that day with a playmate. The family, however, normally attended Mass at St. Boniface's. She confirmed that Alma attended school at the Sisters of Mercy on East Broadway, not St. John's Church.

Weitzel also confirmed that Alma would have had a brand-new handkerchief with a little bowknot in the corner that was not plain but had a crossbar texture in the fabric. It was the only one she owned. Under her dress, she had a white ribbed undershirt and black lingerie. Weitzel's testimony concluded with the agreement that she did not view the remains, nor did she attend the funeral, and that, to her knowledge, neither did Florence Kellner, who had taken to her bed.

Dr. W.B.C. Yont, a druggist, testified that he had seen the child that morning from his business at Hancock and Broadway, within the same block as the Kellner home. He placed the time at twenty minutes to nine, which was, of course, incorrect, as it would have likely been twenty minutes to ten. He agreed that he surmised the time but was certain as to the day. Huffaker attempted to correct Dr. Yont's testimony as to the time but drew an objection. The druggist thought she was coming inside, but she headed north on Hancock instead.

Next on the stand was Mrs. John Valla. She lived on Stephens avenue, near Cherokee Park, at the time of the trial, but at the time of the murder, she lived at First and Green streets, where she was in the business of running a saloon. She testified that she had arrived at the church while services were still going on, in time for the Last Gospel. She described the other two women, along with the child, who were in the church after Mass ended, and said that when she left, about twenty minutes after ten, there were still the two ladies and a young girl, presumably Alma. She described where the girl was sitting in the church, close to the front. She attracted Mrs. Valla's attention because of her obvious devotion. Valla also described the man who came in and placed candles on the altar, she presumed the janitor, and the location of sacristies on either side of the church, in the sanctuary. She stated that the man went back into one of the sacristies. He was the only man she saw in the church at that time. Although she did not know Alma Kellner, the girl had once been part of a crowd of children she'd seen playing at Jackson and Broadway. She admitted that she never saw the child's face, but only saw her from the back, her head and shoulders above the edge of the pew, and that she only supposed the child was Alma Kellner.

Following Mrs. Valla came W.K. Augustus, a letter carrier. He testified that he was well acquainted with Alma as a child in the neighborhood and that she had always "had a word to say" to him when they met. He had encountered her that morning on the west side of Hancock, heading north on Hancock, just north of Clay, and had just gone past Gray street. He was going in the opposite direction, toward Broadway. They shared a "howdy" as they passed.

He was followed on the witness stand by Ann Graele, who lived on Ash street. She had intended to go to the cathedral that morning, rather than attending St. John's, her usual church, and intended to go to the Seelbach afterward to see her son. On the streetcar, she would have passed St. John's. However, realizing she would be late for the cathedral, she decided to attend St. John's instead. On the way there, she encountered Rosa Stauble, with whom she wasn't familiar, and together they walked to the church. She, too, saw the girl at the altar railing in the front of the church on the lefthand side, and then the girl passed over to the right side, nearer Clay street, where she played with the revolving candleholder there. Graele described the checked coat and red hat. She also spotted the tall and slim man, with very dark hair, wearing a coat, who came out of the sacristy on the left side (nearest the inner courtyard) and then immediately went back inside that room. She had observed another man come in through the back of the church, from Walnut street, wearing a dark overcoat, who sat on the other side of the church and left a few minutes later. Stauble was still there when she left a few minutes later. She had realized the following day, when the news was shared about young Alma's disappearance, that she had seen her at the church, so she called the Kellner home to tell them about it. She stated that she had noticed that the child seemed to be waiting for someone and was getting impatient, as she kept glancing over her shoulder and looking to the back of the church.

Elizabeth Dolle also testified. Unlike the other women, she'd been present for the entire Mass, as she was a regular attendee at St. John's and knew that Sunday Mass was at 10:00 a.m. but, on feast days, was at 9:00 a.m. She had observed Alma come in at the end of the service and assumed she was late because she had been playing along the way. She also noted that Alma was "right fidgety." They left the church together, and since it was windy, the child was holding her hat. Dolle noted that she was "just certain almost" that it was Alma Kellner, because she knew Mr. Kellner, and the child resembled him "right smart." They both crossed to the west side of Clay street at Walnut, at which point Dolle headed out onto Clay street and didn't notice her again. She estimated that it was a few minutes before ten at that time.

The last of the ladies at the church to testify was Rosa Stauble, who lived close by the church on Marshall street. It was not her regular church, and she, too, assumed that Mass would be at 10:00 a.m. Having missed Mass, however, she remained to pray for a bit with her rosary and her prayer book. Graele had called her attention to the child at the Communion railing playing with the revolving candlesticks. She arrived home as the clock struck 11:00 a.m., having walked the three squares and a half from the church. The only man she saw in the church was the janitor, and she observed him watching the child. The man had no hat or overcoat and had black hair and a mustache. He had emerged from the sacristy room on the Clay street side. Under cross-examination, she admitted that, as the janitor, he had the right to be around the altar and a right to notice a child playing near the altar. She did not, however, notice any other man in the church.

Father Schuhmann, identified as George William Schuhmann, testified next. He stated that on feast days he served Mass at 6:00 a.m. and 9:00 a.m., and on Sundays, Mass was at 7:00 a.m. and 10:00 a.m. Mass on feast days was earlier, due to it being a working day. He testified that Joseph Wendling had been the janitor at the church for the month prior to the child's disappearance and left without notice on January 14, 1910. He testified, however, that while Wendling was the only janitor, the former janitor, Benedict Thomas, also lived on the premises, even though he had taken different employment.

Father Schuhmann described the duties that Wendling would have been expected to perform. His first duty would have been to stoke up the fire in the church, to warm it before Mass. He would then ring the Angelus bell at 6:00 a.m., which, on feast days, as December 8 was, would have also signaled the start of Mass. If the altar boys had not lighted the candles, Wendling would do that, as well as keep the fires going throughout the morning. At 8:30 a.m. and again at five minutes to 9:00 a.m., he would ring the church bell. At the end of the Mass, he was to close and lock the front door unless there was a reason for the doors to be left open. The only other specific duty Wendling would have had that day would be to keep up the fire throughout the day, as there was a service at 7:30 p.m. that evening.

During the time Wendling worked as the janitor, Father Schuhmann related, he'd always been in good health and had sole charge of the furnaces and was responsible for cleaning. The front doors to the church did not have keys, being kept closed by bars on the inside. The only door into the church from the yard and the rear of the rectory led from the sacristy on that side, and there was no door on the Clay street side at all. The door nearest the rectory was locked, and both the priest and the janitor had a key, possibly two. He described the buildings on the property, which included the church itself, the rectory and the old school building that included the music room. The church was, he described, a "high Church" that seated comfortably seven hundred to eight hundred congregants. He further described the normal arrangement of the altar separated from the pews by the Communion railing and the two sacristy rooms. The one with the door is where the priest would don vestments. The room on the opposite side was used for storage only and had no door, but it did, however, have a hole in the floor. He had never been down all the way into it, but Father Schuhmann had fallen into it once. He was not able to tell how deep it was but stated that "one leg went through it" and he did not touch the ground. He was able to raise himself out of the hole on his own. It served no purpose during the time he was there. He indicated that, originally, there was no basement to the church and that the area eventually created for the furnaces was "cut in" during the time of Father Lawrence Bax, the previous pastor. A double cellar door led from the yard, near the sacristy door, with no key, and steps led down into the cellar, first into a coal room and then into the area with the two furnaces, separated by a mound of dirt. The walls of the room where the furnaces stood, made of hardened clay, were six to seven feet high.

Father Schuhmann went on to describe the rectory, which he shared with the Wendlings. The couple lived in two rooms in the rear of the second floor, which they could access from the regular staircase or from a separate staircase that led down to the kitchen. At the rear of the church property, running from Clay street parallel to Walnut, was the current school building, with a small shed in the eastern corner used for coal, kindling and tools, along with a platform holding old trash and carpet, a "junk room or rummage room, as it were." He agreed that there were several ladders about the place and that, once, he'd purchased lime and sand to repair blackboards.[17]

Father Schuhmann did not know Alma Kellner but did recall having served Mass that day. Right after Mass, he entertained a frequent visitor, Father Cyril Van de Pitte, whom he had known from being stationed together at the cathedral for several years. He noted that Father Van de Pitte came to the rectory several times a week and often took supper with Father Schuhmann on Sunday evenings. Van de Pitte was, he stated, a native of Belgium and had been in the United States for some six years. He had been surprised that day, however, that Van de Pitte wasn't at his own church on the Eighteenth street road, since it was a holy day, but it turned out that Van de Pitte had forgotten about it, having thought it was a day that "Rome had put away with" for the benefit of parishioners who had to work on such days. They shared breakfast, went over some Christmas music and then shared dinner at noon, at which point the visiting priest left.

Father Schuhmann first became aware that Alma Kellner—or, at least, a female child—was missing at about 7:00 p.m., when George Kremer called to ask if he'd seen a "strange man about the place." One of the Mercy teaching sisters then called, asking about any entertainments that day, which Father Schuhmann answered in the negative. He had services at 7:30 p.m., which ended by 8:30. After 9:00 p.m., the doorbell rang. (He answered the door after 9:00 to relieve Lena Wendling of the responsibility.) He found Patrolman Quill at the door, asking if it was possible that the missing child had fallen into the water closet. Father Schuhmann thought that to be impossible, as the water closets (toilets) at the church had bowls, but he invited the patrolman to come to see for himself. Joseph Wendling lit a lamp and accompanied them. Quill searched the area, including the water closet that children would normally have used. He did not recall going down to the furnaces or over to the music room. He testified that he'd asked Wendling at least twice and also announced to the congregation that if they had any information about the child, to contact the police, even giving them the telephone number. Wendling had told him that there were women still in the church when he'd initially planned to close the doors, so he'd waited and went back after they left. Schuhmann believed that Wendling had denied seeing any little girl at the time.

Father Schuhmann was asked about having a discussion with Wendling about a smell in the church earlier in the day. Father Schuhmann expected a large attendance at Mass that evening, so around supper time, he went over to check to see if the church was warm enough. He did not find it warm enough and told Wendling, but he also asked about the odd smell from the register. Wendling explained that he'd burned some old rags and included,

Father Schuhmann thought, that he'd said the rags had oil on them. He did not recall that it was particularly disagreeable, however.

On January 14, he stated, Wendling took "French leave" (leaving without asking permission). Until that time, Wendling had been friendly and courteous. His disappearance was unexpected. His work had been satisfactory. On that day, Frank Fehr had called on the priest between 2:00 and 4:00 p.m., and they sat in the front parlor for a time. He did not know which of the Wendlings had admitted Fehr that day. They walked over to the church, through the sacristy door, which was left unlocked during the day as a rule. He did not recall having seen Joseph Wendling during that time. He last saw Wendling at a funeral he'd handled that morning and only realized that Wendling was missing when he did not perform his expected duties that evening.

Father Schuhmann was questioned about the old school building, which occupied the space to the east of the rectory.[18] The music room in that building was entered from a passageway between the two buildings, through a door that was ten to fifteen feet in from Walnut street. Several steps led up to that door. That room was used as a meeting room. The trapdoor opened into the cellar space, he stated, but did not have any steps down into the space. He believed the space was at least seven to eight feet high, as he could walk in it without stooping. Thomas lived in a room behind that music room, but it had no connection to that room. Thomas continued to stay there after Wendling took over as janitor for some period of time, but for how long, Father Schuhmann couldn't be sure. Thomas returned to work at the church several days after Wendling disappeared. The key to the music room hung in the kitchen, but Lena Wendling was only responsible for the rectory. He had no recollection of Joseph Wendling ever sewing any of the carpet, but he had removed some carpet from the music room at some point during the time he worked at the church and had moved a piece of furniture or carpet to block the trapdoor into the cellar.

Father Schuhmann learned that water had collected in the cellar from Thomas. He made arrangements to have the space pumped out; that process started on May 29, 1910. One of the workmen had explained that he'd gone to school there many years before and that the water from the roof had drained into a cistern there that dated from before the building of the school and that there had been a pump for the water. The plumbers, from Haller & Zehnder, advised that the water be pumped out first. That process started on Saturday morning. Schuhmann saw Richard Sweet working that day, and he returned on Monday morning to continue the process.

Schuhmann was not notified of the discovery of the body, but Lena Wendling told him that policemen were outside. He thought, initially, that they were there to condemn the school building. He rushed to the first officer and was told that a dead body had been found "down there." Father Schuhmann went down into the cellar, which was very dark. George Kremer held a lantern, but Schuhmann saw only a bone and some cloth in the space indicated. He expressed concern about Bax's involvement, as he was connected to St. John's, but the coroner told him that he was a city undertaker. Kremer turned everything over to the coroner to handle. (Father Bax had been the pastor, and a family member ran the family funeral home.)

He identified carpet shown to him as having been used for special occasions at the church, but he did not know where it was normally kept. It was last used at the commencement in June 1909 and was in "fairly good condition." He had next looked for it, and couldn't find it, during Holy Week, before Easter 1910. Thomas subsequently located it in the coal shed in July, and at that time, it was dirty and spotted with what appeared to be blood spots. Schuhmann stated that he could not really identify any of Wendling's clothing.

At this point, it was time for the noon meal. When the court reconvened, it was discovered that Father Schuhmann had not been present when the other witnesses were sworn in, so he was given the oath at that time. He affirmed at that time that all of the answers he'd given before had been truthful. Under cross-examination by John Ray, he stated that he'd met Wendling while the latter was running the elevator at Smith & Nixon's and that Father Van De Pitte had recommended him. When he called upon the Wendlings, he found their home clean and neat, and he found it be a good idea to hire both a cook and a janitor as a couple. He could not tell at any time whether the Wendlings were in their rooms as a rule, because he never occupied his own bedroom until he was ready to go to bed, and that was usually long after the Wendlings had retired for the night. He never entered their rooms while they occupied them. He assumed that the Wendlings were Catholic and that Joseph Wendling attended at least a weekly service from his post in the sacristy. He would only be present at other Masses to turn the lights on and off during the middle of the service. The societies that met at the music room had their own keys and used the books stored in two large bookcases in the room, but Wendling was expected to prepare a fire for them in cold weather. There was also a desk with a lid and a piano in the room. Children would use the room on occasion, as well.

Father Schuhmann testified that he'd made no changes in the space since the body was discovered and that there was still some water in the cellar. He did not know how the water was getting in, but the problem stopped when the body was located. He had been told by the authorities, after the child's body was removed, that he could fill it in or "throw in some disinfectant," but he'd chosen to do nothing to it. He agreed that he may have mentioned making changes in the upper room, making one large room by tearing out the partition, in January. He also agreed that one of the furnaces would smoke on occasion and that he believed both furnaces were in use on December 8, as it was very cold.

Father Schuhmann described how the premises had been searched several times during the days after Alma disappeared, but in a cursory manner.

At that point, the defense attorney stated that he wished to make an investigation and would call Father Schuhmann back. Schuhmann explained that his priestly obligations, a scheduled funeral, might interfere with his return. Answering a last question, he stated that he never accused Wendling, never suspected him and found nothing unusual about his conduct during the time. He confirmed that on January 14 he'd been busy in the afternoon with sick calls and that, when he returned, he was told that Joe had left before supper "with some French troupe." He answered further questions, going back over the same ground covered earlier. He was dismissed and told to report the next morning.

James Payton, the gas meter reader, testified that he'd been calling on the church every month for more than six years and had always used a key that hung in the kitchen to get into the music room. He had first found it missing in December 1909. Not finding the key, he read the meter in the church and the rectory and then asked Lena Wendling for the key. She summoned Joseph Wendling, who told Payton it was unnecessary to read the meter, as they were not using gas there. Payton insisted on reading the meter, however, and Wendling gave in, taking the key from his pocket and letting him in. He stayed with Payton as he read the meter and locked up again. Payton noted that, from that time, he would get the key from the current janitor.

Finally, late in the afternoon, Dr. Ellis Duncan, the county coroner, took the stand. He testified that he became coroner on January 3, 1910. On May 31, 1910, he was called to St. John's concerning a skeleton found in the cellar. It had not been moved and was buried in a shallow place, wrapped in what he later learned was a piece of carpet. That was turned over to Captain Carney. Duncan described how the body was removed to the city undertaker's establishment for examination and the bones cleaned of debris, with everything that washed off carefully examined. The only clothing left with the bones were a partially burned shoe and a stocking found on the left foot of the skeleton. Dr. Ellis detailed how he carefully removed the shoe and stocking from the foot, and he identified the items in court. The other foot was not found with the skeleton, and the hands were never found. He agreed that another foot was found under the church by Richard Hite. He was questioned about how he identified the foot and noted that the two feet corresponded in size and that the second foot found was a right foot, with the lower leg bones, some three to four inches, still attached. It fit closely to the broken end of the corresponding leg bone of the skeleton. What remained was blackened by exposure to fire. Dr. Duncan testified that the ribs of the skeleton were mostly broken, with only two whole ribs remaining. The remainder of the rib cage was broken up and scattered. He was, however, able to find and identify twenty-three ribs, all with the skeleton. He indicated that the entire spine was present and still connected but that only short pieces of rib bones, an inch or so, were left still attached to the spine in several cases.

A large quantity of the skull was missing; only part of the front, the face, was present, the remainder having been cleaved off. He described the damage to the skull in precise anatomical detail to the jury. The skull showed little effect of being exposed to fire but for the edges of the fracture lines, indicating that the outside, not the inside, had been subject to fire. There was no brain tissue present at all, with the inside of the brain cavity being "perfectly clean." The bones of the dorsal spine were the most blackened of all of the vertebrae, with the lowest two in the lumbar section being undamaged. Only a very small strip of skin remained with the torso of the skeleton. He agreed that the corpse had to have been subjected to some other agency to have resulted in the condition in which it was found. He noted that, by all indications, including an assessment of the internal organs, the corpse was that of a female. The state of the small amount of skin found and the hair that had been located with the skull indicated that the child was white. (When Dr. Duncan, however, mentioned that the body was that of a child, Clements objected, at which pointed Duncan changed the term to *corpse*.)

He described the skeleton as being just under four feet long and, when allowing for shrinkage, it would have belonged to a person four to four and a half feet tall. The small foot was seven inches in length. Overall, that corresponded to an estimate of a child between seven and ten years old. He noted that Dr. Ruby, Alma Kellner's dentist, was allowed to examine the few teeth found with the skull and gathered from the debris around the corpse. Properly, Dr. Duncan did not testify as to Dr. Ruby's findings.

Dr. Duncan testified that there was no way to determine the cause of death but noted that the damage to the skull or the chest independently would have proved fatal. Dr. Duncan delicately indicated that, although the child's genitalia were present, it was so damaged by maceration and decomposition that it was impossible to know for sure whether the child had been ravished.

Under cross-examination, Dr. Duncan was questioned and responded in excruciatingly gruesome detail about the soft tissue that remained with the corpse. He explained that much remained of the internal organs, although almost all of the skin and much of the external musculature were missing. He concluded, in a back-and-forth with the defense, and then on re-examination by the prosecutor, that he could simply not speculate as to which of the injuries occurred before the child's death and which were postmortem.

Following the coroner, a number of witnesses testified, adding small details to their prior testimony. Richard Sweet, for example, noted that he'd started the pumping of the cellar on Saturday but, on Sunday, pulled the pipe being used to remove the water temporarily because the church was giving the rite of First Communion to children. He detailed how he'd found the body and fled the church in horror and had immediately called the police station and then his employer. In another detail, he indicated that he and Jacob Haller had to move one of the bookcases in the schoolroom to access the trapdoor into the cellar. On questioning, he indicated that there was no way into the cellar but through the trapdoor and that there was only a small "ventilator" into the space on the Walnut street side.

Sweet also acknowledged that he had applied for a reward but, at the time of the trial, had yet to receive anything. He had, however, received $100 from Frank Fehr.

The shoe salesman, Henry Michael Jr., testified next. He had waited on the Kellner family regularly and recalled having sold Alma a pair of shoes just a month before her death. Shown the shoe found with the corpse, he agreed that it could quite possibly be one he'd sold to the family for her but that, of course, he could not swear to it. He identified the shoe size and noted the mark in the shoe indicating that it was one handled by his business. Under cross, he provided a detailed description of how the shoe store operated and agreed that as a shoe salesman he remembered details about the regular customers, as the Kellners were. A growing child such as Alma Kellner would require new shoes every two months, as a rule.

Next on the witness stand came Benedict Thomas, who had served as the church janitor for almost a year prior to Joseph Wendling's arrival and then returned to the job after Wendling left a month later. On the day of Alma's disappearance, however, he had been working at Smith & Nixon's as an elevator man and an assistant janitor, having started work that day at 7:00 a.m. and remaining under quitting time, 6:00 p.m. He recalled attending Mass that morning and also attending services that evening. He remained at the firm the entire day, except for lunch, which he took at a restaurant on Third street. He agreed that he had continued to live at the church, in the school building, for some time after he had left employment there, but he could not say for sure if he was still living there when Alma disappeared. He was boarding at his sister's, taking his meals there, not at the church. There was no access between the room where he slept and the music room. However, when he left, he did not recall a carpet over the trapdoor, but when he returned, there was one. There was also a heavy Turkish carpet in the room. A desk had been placed over the trap. When he left the position, he had instructed Wendling on how to operate the furnaces and had turned over all of his keys to him. Once he gave up the position as janitor, Thomas had gone down into the furnace area once, perhaps twice, to teach Wendling how to attend to it.

Thomas was familiar with the piece of carpet, as it was used on special occasions and had been clean the last time he had seen it in the little shed in the center of the rear yard. He recalled looking for it at Easter and had initially not located it, but later, on July 19, he discovered it in the coal shed inside the school building. Trash also filled the room. (The shed, as it was called, was in the nature of a loft area suspended between the first and second floors of the building, accessed by a ladder.) He was not looking for it at the time but was instead intending to clean out and burn any unneeded items. When found, it bore dark stains. He told Father Schuhmann of the find, and in turn, Schuhmann called the police and turned it over to Detective Frank Alvin.

Following Wendling's departure, he testified, Lena Wendling had given him a pair of trousers and house slippers that her husband had owned.

Under cross, he agreed that the ashes in the furnace room had been there when he had first taken the position and remained when he returned. He was asked about finding a child's glove earlier in 1909 and stated that it had

Kellner's tooth, he noted her age and that he had to take into consideration the number of children of that age and how "comparatively few have their teeth attended to." Dr. Ruby refused to speculate how many dentists were practicing in Louisville but stated that he had been doing so since 1896 and had filled any number of children's teeth during that time.

The next witness, A.C. Palm, identified himself as a carpet layer. He testified that he had laid carpet at the school and taken up the old carpet. He placed it in time as some two weeks before Father Bax left the church, in 1909. Shown the carpet in evidence, he agreed that it was the old carpet he had removed. The carpet was red and green, with a white figure and a white stripe, and it had faded. Challenged, Palm indicated that he was not in the habit of removing carpet; he usually just laid it. In fact, he indicated, this was the only carpet he had ever had occasion to remove, doing so only because he "had to."

In the face of Clements's obvious doubt that he could remember such detail, Palm noted that "it is very seldom I see a carpet that I don't remember." He had laid carpet of the same character, two-ply, on the stage of the room. He'd left the old carpet on the stage and never saw a janitor and, in fact, "never seen a soul" while he was working. He agreed that he had seen a lot of carpet over the years, but not that color, and he noted that it was the regular pattern for the stage. He agreed that he had seen similar carpet in other places.

Next, Henry Michael Sr., the father of the witness from earlier with the same name, testified. He identified the shoe found as one made in Cincinnati. He stated that his own firm, Volz & Michael, handled that type of shoe, but he could not speculate as to whether any other firms in the city did as well. He testified that when it was found, it was shown to him and he had compared it to other shoes of the same lot in his possession. The markings on the shoe, he stated, indicated that it was made for his store alone. He recognized the number imprinted in the shoe and noted that the shoe was a No. 11 D last. (In testimony moments later, he indicated that the code number reflected an E last, however. A "last" is the mold upon which a shoe is constructed and sized. The letter, then as now, indicates the width of the shoe, and the number indicates the length.) Michael indicated that he felt the shoe he was being shown was missing more material than the shoe he'd been shown in June, but he did believe it was the same shoe. He had examined it carefully at that time. He translated the codes stamped inside the shoe that gave him information about the size. The change in size in the two months between shoes sold on Alma's behalf was consistent, and he also noted that she had likely been wearing "light hose" earlier in the fall.

Patrolman Quill took the stand next. Immediately, Ray objected, saying he thought he had seen Quill in the courtroom previously, which would not have been allowed. Quill denied having been in the room, however, and the court took his word for it.

Quill testified as to his first and second visits to the church, on subsequent nights. He had paid a visit to Father Schuhmann the night Alma was reported missing, he related, and the priest admitted him. Joseph Wendling was present and escorted him through the schoolhouse and to look at the water closets, one for the girls and one for the boys. He admitted that, at the time, he was searching for a dead child. The next night, he returned and, seeing the front of the rectory dark, entered through the passageway between the rectory and the music room, intending to rap on the rear of the building. He encountered Wendling sitting on the steps at the back, and Wendling told the officer that there were many men, police, already there. Wendling unlocked the music building and shined his light inside. The lantern Wendling was using was a "Bull's Eye Dark lantern"—an old-style coal lamp with a door that could be used to adjust the amount of light. Quill admitted that he had gone into the basement of the church but did not make a thorough search. He had not gone into the cellar of the school building or any of the sheds on the property.

Frank Fehr testified next. Although related to Alma, he had not seen her much. He spoke of making a diligent search for the girl but had been at the church only once before he visited on January 14, 1910. He had been inside the sanctuary and spoken to Father Schuhmann while standing close to the sacristy. He spotted a man there "performing the duties of a janitor" but did not notice his face. He discussed the heating system with the priest at the time and acknowledged that he spoke sufficiently loud that the man could have easily overheard everything said. Upon objection by the defense, Judge Gregory admonished the jury that it was up to them to determine if the janitor present was, in fact, Wendling. Under cross-examination, Fehr admitted offering rewards, first for the discovery of the child and then for the arrest and conviction of her killer. Upon avowal, it was agreed that Fehr had gotten several communications from parties claiming they had possession of Alma Kellner. He also testified that they had followed up on every clue and that he had made a trip to Rising Sun, Indiana, among other places, to look at a child thought to be Alma.

He noted that he had not gone to the cemetery, in fact, although the other men reported that he had done so. He had viewed the remains, but the Kellners had not.

Cora Munea took the stand next; Huffaker questioned her. She had been introduced to Wendling, going under the name Henri Jacquemin, in Houston at her aunt's home. He showed her a wound that he claimed he'd gotten as a soldier in Africa and said that he'd been in the United States, specifically New Orleans and New York, for three years. He had conversed with her aunt at length in French, but Munea stated that she was not fluent in it. Wendling claimed, however, to be single. This visit occurred in January 1910, and she had returned home to Missouri about February 2. She received two postcards from him, one from Vallejo, California. He never mentioned Louisville. Under cross, she admitted that while she claimed to be a widow, in fact, she had not seen her husband for ten years and did not know if he was alive or dead.

She was also asked about making a claim for the reward. She stated that she had thought it was for an arrest but did not know that "conviction was attached to it" until told by Captain Carney. She expected to make a claim for it but had yet to take any steps. She was testifying, however, as to the truth.

Detective Sergeant Thomas Burke came next and talked of receiving information concerning Wendling's whereabouts. After ringing the bell for some minutes, Mrs. Moriarty—the landlady—admitted him. He talked to her and showed photographs to her. He set about to search the house, with Detective Ryan standing by. Upstairs, he checked several rooms. Wendling then emerged from a water closet. He was wearing a hat, an undershirt, under-drawers, pants and untied shoes. On being asked, he gave his name as Jacquemin, admitting that he also went by Wendling and that he was a deserter from the French army.

Burke testified concerning the arrest and questioning, done in the presence of the chief of police and the district attorney. Wendling claimed that he left due to his wife, who would take his wages and give them to her brother. He stated that he shaved his mustache because a girl "down South" did not like it. He also admitted that he had known for some eight weeks that there was a reward offered for his arrest. On further questioning, Burke stated that Wendling admitted having seen Alma several times and that his responses were given freely and voluntarily. By that time, Captain Carney had arrived, and they all went in to talk to Wendling. The captain "sized him up," and Wendling admitted he knew who the Louisville officer was. Carney explained that there was an indictment from Kentucky; Wendling agreed to "go back without papers," stating, "I am pure and I am willing to go back." He stated that he understood what the "papers"—extradition—were.

Curiously, Wendling was questioned about the clothing he had in his possession, which included two ladies' handkerchiefs, two pairs of gloves, two ladies' pairs of gloves, a pair of ladies' stockings and a pair of ladies' drawers. He also had a "net undershirt" that was for ladies. He also had some face paint in his belongings. The police turned everything over to Captain Carney.

During cross, Burke denied having any intention to make a claim for any reward, despite what had been reported publicly. He admitted that some items in Wendling's possession had been sent to Vallejo, having been stolen from there—the items included the women's clothing and a stickpin.

The court recalled Father Schuhmann. He denied that any carpet was ever kept on the floor of the room where the trapdoor was located and that a roll of carpet in evidence was normally kept in a storeroom. He also admitted that a statue in relief in the church had been retouched by a painter who used a number of colors. The painter did quite a few statues, some before and some after the discovery of the body, which caused him to pause in his work.

Father Schuhmann was questioned about the church rule with respect to re-consecration of a church after a violent crime, but the prosecutor objected to that question and to any question about whether the church had been so re-consecrated. The judge sustained the objections. The priest did identify a piece of fabric shown to him by Loraine Mix as being a cover for a candlestick.

Peter Herbst was called to the stand next. He claimed to have delivered lime and sand to the church during cold weather, to Joseph Wendling, and that Lena Wendling paid him for it.

William Kammerer was recalled; he was asked about the items that were found in the basement of the church. He identified each by the envelope in which it was contained, and it was marked as evidence. He authenticated each of the items he had found. Once identified, they were turned over to the court stenographer. Detective Simons was also recalled; he, too, testified about the items he had collected from the scene.

Dr. Vernon Robins was called by the prosecution and identified himself as the city chemist and bacteriologist, as well as a physician. He identified the teeth found and approximated the age of the child—taking into consideration the normal emergence of the teeth—as between eight and nine years old.

He testified as to the stains on a piece of carpet as being both charcoal and decomposed blood. The carpet also included lime in powder form and hair that had been exposed to heat. He found blood and urine stains on the undershirt found in the belfry closet. He had tested Wendling's clothing found in his rooms and noted that there was blood on his swimming trunks and on one of his shirts. He found blood and muscle fiber on a knife, as well. Dr. Robins also discussed all of the handkerchiefs and pieces of cloth found in the basement, previously authenticated by the two officers; he reported that some of the items had not actually been tested, according to his records. Some did contain blood and muscle fiber. Under cross, he admitted that he could not tell if the blood was from an adult or a child or if the blood from several people were represented. He stated definitively, however, that it could not be period blood from a woman and described the difference in such blood on the microscopic level. He affirmed that it was also, for certain, human rather than animal blood and agreed that some could have been from a nosebleed. He described in detail the chemical process used in testing the samples, which involved the use of a solvent to dissolve the stain.

Dr. Duncan was also recalled. He affirmed that all of the bones were from the same skeleton, even though they were found at different times and in different places.

Finally, Captain John Carney took the stand. He described where he'd gone to find Wendling: "I went into Houston, Texas; Houston Texas to San Antonio; San Antonio to Delling [sic] Ranch; Delling Ranch back to Houston; Houston to Galveston; Galveston back to San Antonio. It would take me a week to tell you all the places I have been in."

He discussed a conversation with Wendling, in the presence of Detective Sergeant Burke and Officer Ryan, and agreed that Wendling spoke "voluntarily without duress or compulsion of any kind." He had asked if Wendling would "waive papers" and ensured that Wendling understood what that meant. He noted that Wendling agreed to return and said "when I go back I will tell who done it." He cautioned Wendling that what he said could be used against him and not to "talk too much." He agreed that he took possession of some of Wendling's possessions and that others were held in San Francisco as evidence. Carney identified photographs of the items described previously by Burke. They were pinned to a line for the purpose of being photographed. He also described the search of the Wendlings' room and the items found in a basket hamper. He had first learned of the child's disappearance between 9:00 and 11:00 p.m. on December 8. He described the search that began the morning of December 9, 1909, and didn't end until the body was discovered. "I made a diligent search, sent posters broadcast, had circulars sent all over the universe, had telephone communications made within a radius of two hundred miles, had boats apprehended or overhauled on both ends of the river, every train and interurban car leaving this city was communicated with."

When asked about the possibility of claiming any reward, Carney responded: "I waived my right, as far as the state of Kentucky is concerned, with Mr. Todd, the Secretary of State, or the Auditor of the State, I should say."

Carney denied finding any of the items but admitted, for the first time, that he had been in the cellar of the church prior to May 31, staying only briefly because there was no light down there. He had entered secretly and used matches to look around briefly and then left. He introduced several letters that officers had found, including a "character letter" from the French army. Michael Hermann, who had apparently translated the letters and who was in the courtroom, spoke up, but Mix objected to his statements, as he was not the witness.

During the trial, a letter from Lena Wendling to her parents-in-law, and their response, were placed into the records. Her conflicted letter, dated April 1, 1910, read:

Dear Parents:

Nearly three months gone, and no one word. One must have a very cold heart to do this.

Dear Mother, where is my Joseph? Tell where he is. He should come to me. I have no rest day and night. Did he never write to you since he is gone? Tell me where he is.

How are you all? I always said to Joseph to think of his parents, and let us make money together. But he always replied that he is alone and nobody could take anything from him.

He was after me for my money. My money does not run away. We ought to work in order to make money together.

Dear mother, I will forget everything if he comes back. Dear parents answer soon. I send this letter and kiss you with my whole heart.

Mad. Wendling.

Their undated reply read as follows:

Dear Madelene:

It took me quite a while to write you because I was sick with bronchitis and was down three weeks. I hope you are better now. You must not undermine your health for you need it. But it is always very sorrowful.

Perhaps Joe was lured away some place and locked up. May God bring us back poor Joseph.

My dear Madelene we received the money you sent us, and thank you so much for it. Now we can have the roof fixed. If Joe could help us it would do us much pleasure.

Joseph is perhaps at Nagham.

My dear Madelene I have always the idea that he will come back. The father is much annoyed to learn about our child, and to know such things. What bad luck we have. His friends send him their best regards, but I never say anything to them, just thank them.

Madelene, we embrace you, your mother and father who love you. Hope you have news soon.

Henrietta and Edward Wendling.

The questioning on cross went back and forth between what had occurred in San Francisco and the search of the church cellar. Carney noted that Wendling had denied having any bloodstained clothing, although he later claimed he did own the clothing on which stains were found. At that point, Captain Carney said, Wendling was directed to stop answering questions by his attorney.

Reverend Cyril Van de Pitte came to the stand. He had known Father Schuhmann for some years and had married Joe and Lena Wendling two years before, at St. Peter's Roman Catholic Church, then at Sixteenth and Southgate streets. He recommended Wendling to Father Schuhmann to be the janitor. He also visited the rectory on December 8, had dinner and did some singing. At the time, Father Van de Pitte resided at Twenty-Third and Bank streets. He did not recall seeing Wendling that day.

At this point, one of the jurors wished to ask Fred Kellner some questions, and the court recalled him to the stand. The juror confirmed that Kellner had not viewed the remains or attended the funeral but that he accepted the remains as his daughter. The court, however, noted that the question was improper and admonished the jury not to consider it.

The prosecution closed its case, and the defense made an opening statement, not recorded in the official transcript, as it was not evidence. Joseph Wendling came to the stand in his own defense. He identified himself as Henri Joseph Wendling and that he came to the country with a woman, later his wife, Madeline, whom he had met in Germany. He described all the places he had worked since his arrival and how he had progressively learned enough English, changing jobs every few months. He was encouraged to take the job at St. John's by the two priests and described his duties there, tending to the church and ringing the bell at designated times, before Mass and occasionally in the evenings before a prayer service.

Wendling absolutely denied laying his hands on, raping or killing Alma Kellner. He denied hacking or burning her. He struggled to answer some questions, however, given his limited grasp of English. He denied having ever seen her. Part of his duties included closing and locking the doors of the church, and he recalled closing the doors by 10:30 a.m. or so that day, after he confirmed that no one was left in the church. He stated, however, that the side door toward the rectory was left open until he locked it at 8:00 p.m. The first he had learned that the child was missing was at about 9:00 p.m., when the first officer came to the rectory, and he helped in searching the buildings. Although he saw the ashes on the ledges, he claimed he did not touch them but disposed of the daily ashes by putting them out for the city trash man to collect.

Wendling described the carpets that he had found around the school. Father Schuhmann had told him to fix up the music room as best he could. He related how the key to the music building was kept in various places. Others did have keys as well. He claimed that the knife found in his room was one used by his brother-in-law to get a nail out of his horse's foot. The blood on his clothing, he thought, may have come from falls off a bicycle, as he used to race in France. He had also accidentally shot himself in the hand, and some of the blood likely came from that.

He related his troubles with his wife over money, complaining that she "all the time want to be the boss" and would not give him money. On the day he left Louisville, he went to the bank, withdrew all of the money on account and returned to the rectory. He claimed that he never saw Frank Fehr on January 14, and he did not tell his wife he was leaving. When he did leave, he went to the Louisville & Nashville train station and asked the cost of a ticket to San Francisco. When told it was $56.00, he thought that was a little much, as he needed to buy some clothing as well. He decided that going to New Orleans, for $18.50, was a better idea. He found there, however, that he could not get a job, so he proceeded to Houston, making friends with another Frenchman along the way. He worked there for a few weeks and met Cora Munea. Although he spent time with her, he denied proposing marriage.

He left Houston for Galveston, finding that his meager wages did not allow him to keep up with his new friend, who was wealthy. Wendling could not find work there, as he was not a citizen, so he went west to San Antonio and hired on to work on a ranch. However, the hard work of plowing was more than he cared to do for the wages. Finding passage for twenty-five dollars to San Francisco, he left. On the train, he struck up an acquaintance with several people and corresponded with several young ladies he met after he arrived. Arriving in San Francisco, he made his home mostly at the boardinghouse, where police made the arrest.

He immediately got a job with Mr. Wiedmann as a houseman in Vallejo, where he worked for two months. As to the women's clothing in his valise, he explained that he was holding it for a young lady who had too much clothing; she was to reclaim it later. He found another job driving a mail stage from Olema, but he became bored and again returned to the boardinghouse. He never had a chance to get another job, having discovered that he was wanted while in Olema. Following his arrest, he testified, the officers tried to get a wagon but ended up bringing him to the station on a streetcar. He claimed to not understand what extradition was, stating, "A policeman can bring you anyplace." He complained that while Captain Carney was very nice, taking him to the dining car and giving him cigars, the police chief swore at him all the time. (In fact, he apparently meant Colonel John Whallen.) He claimed that he had demanded to be brought straight to Louisville, but they stopped in St. Louis. Several questions about the court hearing there confused Wendling, with his limited language skills, and he stated that he did not ask for an attorney and was alone when being questioned.

Wendling testified that he was afraid when he realized Carney was removing him from the train at half past four o'clock in the morning and made a lot of noise at the time. The officers took him to Evansville. Wendling explained that when taken back to the train station, the officers gave him a cushion.

And Judge Gregory again adjourned the court.

The next morning, Wendling continued his testimony. He acknowledged that the face cream and tonic were his and that he had his picture taken and shared it with various women he met in his travels.

On cross, Huffaker took him back over the same topics. Wendling admitted that the side door into the church could be seen from the kitchen window. Huffaker pressed him, finally drawing an objection about putting words in Wendling's mouth. Huffaker replied, "I don't want to put words in his mouth. He has enough in his mouth without my putting them in it." Attorney Robbins further complained that Huffaker was addressing his client as Wendling, rather than Mr. Wendling.

Wendling complained that before they came to the church, his wife never gave him control of any money. He said, however, that after they were employed at the church, she gave him all of the money, including the ten dollars Father Schuhmann had given her for Christmas. Despite saying that he got along with his wife much better after they no longer lived with her brother, that was when he left her, Huffaker noted. Wendling stated that after they left Alois Arnold's home, he never spoke to him again. He stated that he had wanted to run away but could not do so, as he lacked money.

After going over in detail his prior testimony, once again, Wendling left the stand.

He was followed by several witnesses on his behalf; some had been prosecution witnesses and were recalled. Katie Kavanaugh, a member of the Altar Society, described the process used for items left behind in the church and confirmed having seen a child's gauntlet glove and handkerchiefs in the basket where such items were routinely kept for retrieval. She admitted that she did not know what became of the items but had not noticed any of them being bloody, only soiled. She claimed that such items were often thrown down the hole in the sacristy, however, and people assumed that they would end up in the furnace, but she never went down there herself.

Alois Arnold testified about his brother-in-law. He admitted that Wendling had loaned him a knife and that he used it on his horse's hoof. He explained how they had argued and how he had pulled a pistol on Wendling, and that he wanted to kill him at the time. Huffaker challenged him with testimony from the coroner's inquest; he claimed that he did not testify there, only before the grand jury.

The physician who attended him after the shooting, James C. Morrison, testified about treating his gunshot wound. He noted that Wendling had bled profusely during the process. John Kippes Jr., the brother of Arnold's deceased wife, testified that he was not present when the pair had a

12
THE APPEAL

Wending was now, officially, a man convicted of murder. But, maintaining his innocence, he filed an appeal to his conviction from the Jefferson Circuit Court to the Kentucky Court of Appeals—at the time the highest court in the state and the "court of last resort." J. Reginald Clements and John W. Ray continued their representation of Joseph Wendling in the appellate court. Joseph Huffaker and Loraine Mix, along with James Breathitt, the Kentucky attorney general, and Tom B. McGregor, an assistant attorney general, argued the case for the commonwealth.

Attorneys argued the appeal on March 16, 1911, in Frankfort. The news noted that the case attracted much interest in that city, as well as in Louisville. Through her mother, Alma Kellner had many relatives in Frankfort.

On May 11, 1911, Justice John D. Carroll entered the opinion of the Kentucky Court of Appeals. In its decision, the court observed that Joseph Wendling was a native and citizen of France. Summarizing, the court began its decision by noting that Wendling came to the United States in 1907 and settled in Louisville. He had soon married a woman who had accompanied him to the United States. He was subsequently charged and convicted of the murder of Alma Kellner.

The court then moved on to address the issues under appeal. When the case was called for trial, Wendling, through his counsel, had moved the trial court to grant him the right of a "jury de medietate linguae." The trial court denied the motion.

Following the same legal ground as had been covered by the trial court and in the U.S. District Court, the justices looked to Section 2254 of Carroll's

Kentucky Statutes, the predecessor to the Kentucky Revised Statutes in place today. In the chapter relating to jurors, the law provided for such a right. The court agreed, however, that this law was the "first time presented to this court for its consideration." As the trial court had indicated, there was very little case law throughout the country interpreting the provision in those states that also had a similar provision in their own states' laws. A jury of medietate linguae—a jury of "half tongue"—was defined as one that is composed half of citizens of the state in question and half of aliens, presumably of the same nationality of the defendant. By an ancient custom of the English Parliament, an alien was permitted to claim a jury made up in that way, as a matter of right, in both criminal and civil cases. Although the concept had been carried forward into the law of at least some jurisdictions in the United States, it appeared that the use of such a jury had "grown into nonuse in England" long before the law even came into being in Kentucky. The court noted, "The fact that a law so antiquated and obsolete should be found incorporated in the statutes of this state may well be regarded as one of the curiosities of legislation." The court traced the history of the statute backward, finding that it appeared in the General Statutes adopted in 1873, the Revised Statutes from 1854 and as far back as the statutes from 1796 found in volume 1 of Littell's Laws. (Littell's Statute Law of Kentucky was the first critically edited compilation of Kentucky's law.) The statute came from Virginia, the state from which Kentucky had been carved soon after the American Revolution.

The court noted: "It will then be seen that a law for which there was never any reason in the jurisprudence of the state has been retained from its earliest history in every compilation of the statutes. It stands now and has always stood apart from all other sections of the statute relating to the selection of juries, and has never had any orderly connection with the elaborate system of laws treating of this subject."

The court agreed that the privilege was "contrary to the spirit of American institutions and the public policy of this country." The court could find "no good reason" for according such unusual rights to aliens. However, since it was in fact in the codified statutes of Kentucky, the court found that it must, at least, consider the law, even though the right was "not guaranteed either by the Constitution or by the common law." The Kentucky Court of Appeals acknowledged that the right appeared to originate with a desire in the early history of England to encourage emigration and that, although it was unnecessary in the current circumstances, it lingered on in the compilation of the statutes.

The court recognized that the right to trial by jury was preserved in the current version of the Kentucky Constitution, dating from 1891, with Section 7 stating that "the ancient mode of trial by jury shall be held sacred, and the right therof remains inviolate, subject to such modifications as may be authorized by the Constitution." The essential features of a trial by jury were the right to have a panel of twelve men and that all should agree on the verdict. The qualifications or the mode of the selection of the jurors were not addressed by the state constitution and were left to be developed in the statutory law.

At its core, however, the issue to be resolved was whether the jury de medietate linguae was an actual right, when requested, or a privilege that was left to the discretion of the trial judge. The Kentucky Court of Appeals emphasized the use of the word *may* in the statute and agreed that it was discretionary on the part of the trial judge. As such, Wendling was not, therefore, entitled to a jury made up half of Frenchmen.

Another error complained of by Wendling was the use of an array of special jurors summoned for the day. These jurors were not, he argued, selected as provided by Kentucky law at the time, which required that the jury commissioners in person copy names of potential jurors from the assessor's book. Instead, another individual did so, not under the direct control of the commissioners. As discussed in the case of *Louisville, Henderson & St. Louis Railway Co. v. Schwab*, 105 S.W. 110 (1907), jury selection at the time required the appointed jury commissioners to "write the names of the jurors on slips of paper and place them in the cylinder or wheel, and that, if this service was performed by clerks or others, it was ground of challenge to the panel, and, upon it being made to appear by affidavit or proof that the jury was not selected by the commissioners in the manner provided by law, the panel should be discharged." However, Wendling's motion was not supported by any such proof, and there was a presumption that the jury commissioners, as officers of the court, had performed their duties properly. As such, the appellate court agreed that the trial court was correct in denying the motion when it lacked sufficient proof.

A third claimed error involved the testimony of Frank Fehr at trial as to the events of January 14, 1910. On that day, he spoke to Father Schuhmann at the church. Fehr testified that he did not recognize Wendling in the church that day, although he did see someone performing janitorial duties. However, the trial court permitted Fehr to testify as to his conversation with the priest and that the conversation, it was believed, was overheard by Joseph Wendling and spurred his precipitate flight. Flight, of course, was and is often considered evidence of guilt. Wendling's counsel objected, arguing that it was not even proven the Wendling was present, but the trial judge carefully admonished the jury as to the use of the testimony in its consideration. The appellate court agreed that the testimony was "competent and relevant," since Father Schuhmann had testified that Wendling was the only person who was performing janitorial duties at the church at that time. It agreed that that was sufficient to submit the evidence to the jury. Such timely admonitions, however, were not, legally, instructions, which are given at the end of the trial, but are instead within the purview of the trial judge when believed necessary to ensure that the jury understands its responsibilities.

The court of appeals disposed of additional minor issues. The court agreed that it was proper for the trial judge to refuse to allow Dr. Duncan to testify as to the horrifying discovery of a number of decomposed bodies that had been found during May and June 1910 in public dumps around the city. The court noted that while it was true that such body parts were found, none of those bodies and body parts were found in the basement of the church, or any such building, in fact. (The body parts were, apparently, detritus from local medical schools, which at the time often actively sought out cadavers for study and were not particularly diligent in the proper handling of the remains when they were no longer of use to the students.) As such, the court agreed it was irrelevant evidence and properly excluded. It also found it to be proper to refuse to permit questions to Father Schuhmann about the lack of any re-consecration of the church following the crime. It had been indicated that the canon law of the Catholic Church required that if a church was desecrated by the commission of a violent crime, it was necessary that it be re-consecrated before Mass could be celebrated in it. There had not been, apparently, any such re-consecration of St. John's. The court agreed that there was not even the most remote connection of this information to the crime or the defendant.

Wendling's counsel also raised the issue of its request to examine the articles of evidence prior to the trial. As the court was unaware of any legal mandate that the commonwealth do so, and because the items were freely available for examination during the trial, it agreed that the trial court's decision to deny the opportunity to defense counsel was proper. The court then reviewed a statement made by Wendling, voluntarily, in the presence of witnesses that "if I did kill that girl, nobody saw me but God and he can't come down and tell it. I am pure. I am innocent. I will go back without papers, and, when I go back, I will tell who done it. Me kill no little girl. If I did kill her, nobody saw me do it but God, and he can't come down and tell it." It noted that it was arguable whether the statement rose to the level of a confession and, as such, whether it required a jury instruction to the effect that such a confession, "unless made in open court, will not warrant a conviction, unless accompanied with other proof that such an offense was committed."[19] Wendling's counsel had argued that the trial court should not have given such an instruction, presumably on the thought that it amounted to at least a suggestion to the jury that it was a confession. The trial court, however, in an abundance of caution, had provided a carefully crafted instruction that *if* the jury believed it was a confession, the rule would apply. The appellate court agreed that, if anything, this instruction was beneficial, not prejudicial, to Wendling.

The final issue addressed by the Kentucky Court of Appeals was Wendling's argument that he was denied a public trial. During the trial, it proved necessary for the court to station policemen around the courtroom, at convenient locations, to preserve order and prevent overcrowding. Admission to the courtroom was limited to the number it could comfortably accommodate. (Historically, it was very common for the courtroom to have so many observers that it was standing room only, with some even sitting in the deep windowsills.) At no time during the trial was there any complaint from Wendling that any of his friends and supporters who were interested in his behalf were excluded specifically, nor was there any indication of "favoritism or partiality" by the officers tasked with the responsibility of admitting or excluding those wanting to attend. The court agreed that the decision to limit admission, to preserve order, did not infringe on any constitutional right. The court agreed that Section 11 of the Kentucky Constitution recognized the right of a public trial, but that did "not mean that all of the public who desire to be present shall have opportunity to do so or that the trial judge may not without favor or discrimination limit the spectators to the capacity of the room in which the trial is had." So long as a reasonable proportion of the public "is suffered to attend," the requirement is properly satisfied.

With that, the Kentucky Court of Appeals affirmed Wendling's judgement of conviction. In July, J. Reginald Clements put it about that he was contemplating a petition for certiorari to the U.S. Supreme Court, but eventually, it was decided not to do so. To petition the Supreme Court, Wendling would need the assent of the Kentucky Court of Appeals, but that was not considered an obstacle. In October, Wendling announced that he had fired Clements, but Clements, when asked, denied that that was the case.

13
THE PRISON

Following his conviction, deputies quickly transported Wendling to the prison, and he settled down into life behind bars. Wendling started his incarceration at the state prison on the banks of the Kentucky River, in Frankfort. (This prison was closed soon after the 1937 flood, which necessitated the evacuation of the prison, and it has since been razed.)

During his first year of incarceration, Wendling had few visitors, with only his attorney, Clements, and his wife, accompanied by a Mr. and Mrs. McGinnis, coming to speak to him. The warden quickly dispelled rumors that Wendling had sent a letter to someone admitting complicity in the crime. Warden E.E. Mudd stated that guards read all letters sent by Wendling before being mailed; in the few letters he sent, there was nothing that could be construed as a confession. During his first few years there, Wendling became an accomplished electrician and, eventually, a radio technician as well.

Wendling also amused himself, translating some French verse that he thought "appropriate to his own condition." It read, in part:

> *Don't be too quick to condemn me*
> *Because I was one victims of circumstances*
> *Remember you see but the surface and known not what's in the heart*
> *I may bear the marks of a sinful life*
> *And I may have been a bit wild*
> *But back of it all remains in fact*
> *That I, even I, am God's child.*

Not forgotten in his native country, in December 1915, a rumor appeared in Paris, France, that Wendling had escaped from prison. However, when asked about it, he "said he had not even thought of attempting to escape, and prison officers said he is one of the best prisoners in the institution." He was serving as the prison electrician at the time, a position of high responsibility. It was believed that the rumor arose as a result of an incident in which he was temporarily "missing"—could not be found—when he was wanted to handle a problem and that this was overheard and misunderstood by visitors in the prison. In fact, he was simply behind the stage at the chapel. A few years later, in April 1918, Wendling assisted in searching for another prisoner who was attempting to escape; Wendling gave the alarm and pulled the man out of his hiding place by the seat of his pants.

On August 22, 1919, however, at about 7:00 a.m., Wendling did escape from the Frankfort penitentiary. He asked permission in the electrical shop, where he was working, to go see the warden and was given consent. Instead of going there, however, he donned overalls in the tool room, shouldered a toolbox and then walked to the stockade fence on the north side of the prison. He called to C.C. Stith, the guard on that wall, that he had been sent to repair an electrical problem with the lighting. When Captain Stith lowered a ladder for Wendling's use, he climbed up. When Stith's back was turned, Wendling lowered the ladder on the outside of the fence, climbed down and simply walked away. When another guard spotted and challenged Wendling, the prisoner, on his way out Holmes street, told them he was headed to the prison farm to do some repair work. Since the guards recognized him as an electrician, they did not immediately become suspicious.

It turned out that the prison had dispatched Wendling in the past to perform repair work in the old capitol building nearby, but always with a prison employee accompanying him. He was often left alone to the actual work, however. At one time, the warden had received a complaint that at a home where Wendling had done some work he was exhibiting behavior that caused alarm to the lady of the house. During his time working at the private home, for one of the prison contractors, Wendling had paid far too much attention to the seven-year-old daughter of the homeowner, arousing concern. Because of the complaint, the warden ordered him back to work in the shop inside the prison and revoked many of the "little privileges that he had been given for good behavior." This, the warden believed, triggered Wendling's desire to escape. Since many of the prison guards were unaware of his change in status, they did not attempt to stop him when he was spotted outside the fence. Within a half hour, the prison authorities realized he had escaped and started a search in earnest. The prison swore in a number of citizens as special officers to aid the few prison guards available and the local police. They started the search in the valley that sat to the north of the prison, which was considered the best route for those making a prison break to get out of the city. Captain C.V. Mullikin of the Lexington police was summoned to the scene with his renowned bloodhounds. The dogs were put on the trail first at Wendling's cell and then to the place where he went over the wall. The dogs followed the trail to an old stone house in the valley, but no further. Captain Mullikin stated that Wendling had likely changed shoes or was walking barefoot.

Warden T.M. Pythian believed that Wendling had little money in hand, as he quickly spent his available money, which he earned through his electrician work and doing other odd tasks, on "eggs, fruit and other delicacies." As word spread of the escape, Frankfort citizens joined the search. A reward was posted for a total of $200 for his capture, with $100 from the state for the return of any prisoner and an equal amount from the state board of prison commissioners. Tragically, during the search, one of the extra guards, sworn in from among available citizens, Robert W. Herald, died when his gun fell from his holster and accidentally discharged after he stooped to look under a train freight car.

As the search went into the second day, it was speculated that Wendling had fled after unsuccessfully trying to see little Margaret Doyle, the daughter of the woman who had complained of his behavior to the warden. The mother had received several telephone calls that were apparently a pretext to get her to depart the home and leave her daughter alone there. The prison believed initially that Wendling lacked any access to a telephone to have made such calls, but it learned that the shop in which he had been working, the chair factory, did have one in the office. Mrs. Doyle had earlier received a letter to induce her to go to the capitol, near her home, which was followed by a visit to her home by a man resembling Wendling. The letter appeared to be on stationery used in the chair factory and written on a typewriter with the same type. The child, however, was away on a camping trip at the time. The prison found a telephone book in the office opened to the page on which her name was listed.

Warden Pythian received two tips on August 23, a Saturday, both from women who believed they'd given Wendling breakfast, one in Harrodsburg, in Boyle County, and the other in Stamping Ground, in Scott County. The warden did not believe, however, that Wendling was present at either instance, given the distances involved. The railroads and pikes out of

Frankfort were guarded, and patrols were sent into the hills, to no avail. The warden speculated that Wendling had to have had an accomplice to aid in his escape.

A better tip, however, came from Mrs. H.S. Wash, who lived in the east end of Frankfort. She had fired a shot at a man loitering in her alley who was dressed in a woman's wrapper and wearing a shawl around his head. Police had responded to the scene when she called; as they arrived, the man darted out and fled. Police and citizens took up the trail, which led into the railroad yard. Other witnesses reported seeing the oddly dressed man as well, and all were confident that he existed.

Wendling remained free through the next day as well, and every police department within one hundred miles of Frankfort was alerted. Seaports were provided with information, given the likelihood of Wendling attempting to leave the country. Tips led prison guards to Lockport and Bethlehem, in Henry County, but the calls were fruitless. "Twenty prison guards and civilians are beating the hills back of the State Capitol," but they could not find Wendling.

On August 26, 1919, the newspaper reported that Wendling had been located. He had reportedly tried to break into the home of C.E. Newman, in Frankfort, at about midnight, and Newman had fired a pistol at the intruder. Newman's daughter had spotted a man peeping through her window and screamed, alerting her father. The person ran into an alley, turned onto Main street and was walking in the direction of the post office when Frankfort patrolman Scott spotted him and recognized him, having previously been a guard at the prison. Wendling had a revolver and a knife, the first of which he attempted to draw. Scott struck him with his club, causing a scalp wound that was dressed at the prison when he was returned. According to the tale that Wendling later shared with the warden, only once did he make it beyond the Frankfort city limits. He had tried several roads leading out of the city but turned back when he spotted prison officials searching for him. Wendling reported that he had left his hiding place in the wooded hills, beyond the tunnel, to try to get across the river to the Louisville pike. He reported that guards had been very near his hiding place several times.

His hiding place, his lair, had been, in fact, the attic of the Old Capitol, where he had been working on the electricity in the past.[20] Searching that location, officers found the woman's clothing that he'd been wearing when spotted Friday night, as well as "cornbread, meat and tomato catsup," along with some laundry he'd stolen from an old lady who'd left her basket on Madison Street, near the capitol grounds. Along with some food and the

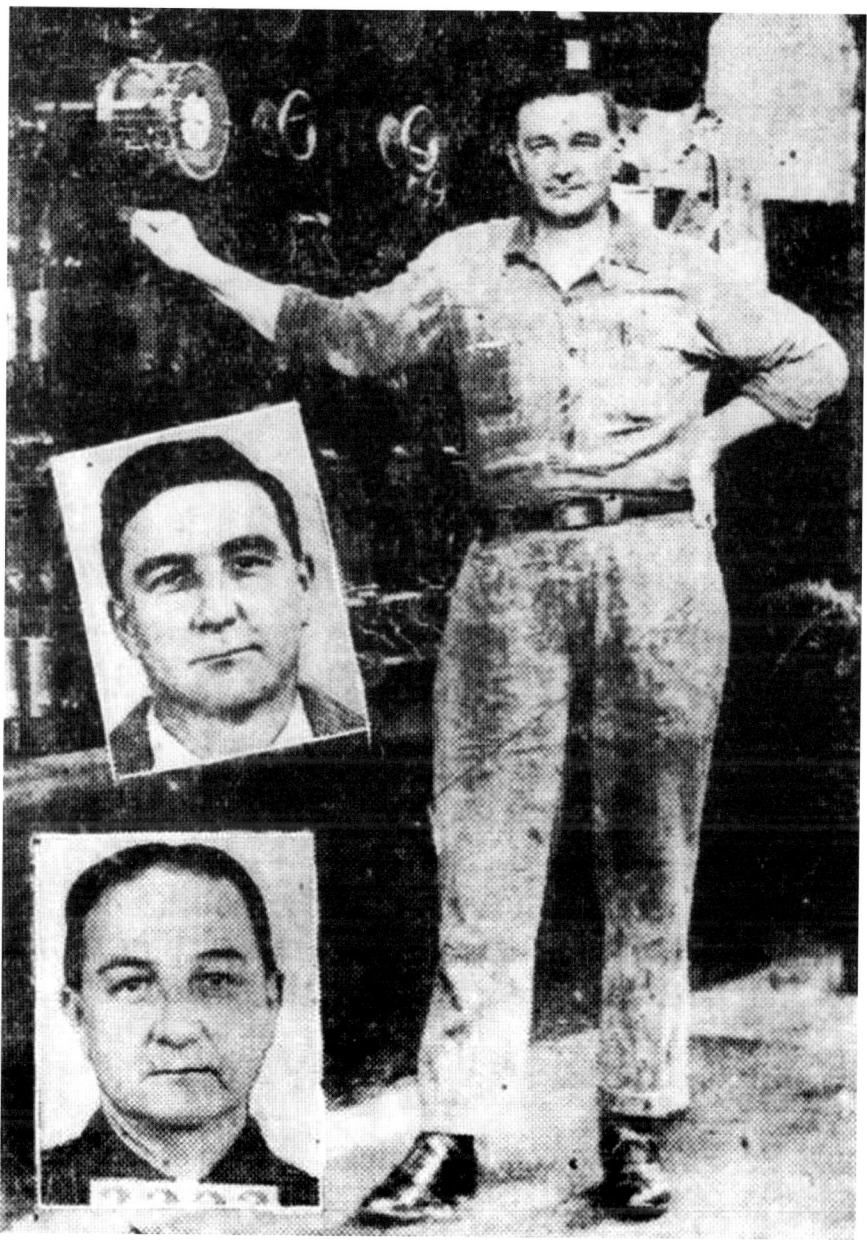

Joseph Wendling in the machinery room of the Kentucky State Penitentiary (Eddyville, Kentucky), as published in the *Courier-Journal*.

missing laundry, the basket now included a woman's raincoat, a wig and a pink veil, as well as the striped cap normally worn by guards, which he had been wearing when he fled. The investigators believed the outfit and the wig were used in plays at the reformatory. Patrolman J.P. Stafford found the items, but the reward for Wendling's capture, it was said, would go to Patrolman O.C. Scott.

Wendling was indicted for his escape, but given his life sentence, the only penalty could be a loss of privileges. Therefore, because of his jaunt, Wendling lost all privileges, and the warden placed him in "third class" and back in the prison stripes, one step lower than "the meanest killer" entering the prison. His hair was cut short, and he was provided with a ball and chain.

In February 1921, Wendling committed a second escapade, when he scaled the wall and then came around to the prison gate, wrapped in a woman's pink kimono and carrying the rope. Although the warden denied that he had been discovered to have gone missing this time, he was suspected of being the mysterious "woman in black" that people had been seeing around town. The county judge, N.B. Smith, and the mayor, William S. Rosson, paid the warden a visit. They concluded that, to allay public fears, the state would transfer Wendling to the state prison at Eddyville. The news reported that "no matinee idol could have attracted more attention than Wendling received at the station" when he was placed on the train. They hoped that the walls at Eddyville would "be high enough to discourage his wanderlust." He and his guard on the trip, D.W. Cannon, arrived too late in Louisville on February 9 to catch the scheduled noon Illinois Central train, so they walked the streets of Louisville for eight hours while waiting for the next train. They caught the 8:45 p.m. train. A few people recognized Wendling at the station, likely to his great pleasure.

Once he arrived in Eddyville, Wendling appealed for assistance to Antonin Bartelemy, the French consul in Chicago, asking for assistance in gaining a parole. Although the consul sent an inquiry to the state board of charities and corrections, it was to no avail. Oddly, the prison listed Wendling's age as sixty-one, but he claimed to be only fifty, which was consistent with him having been twenty-seven at the time Alma Kellner was murdered.

14
THE PAROLE

fter some seven years at Eddyville, Joseph Wendling continued to seek a parole. In 1928, in a letter dated August 2, he pled his case to *True Detective* magazine in New York City.

Dear Sir—

I am writing you this letter to find out if you will do me a favor.

I am an inmate of the Kentucky State Penitentiary at this town, am serving a life sentence for conviction that was handed down by the jury of Jefferson County, Kentucky, for the murder of this little girl that is the center of topic in your story titled: The Crime that Rocked a Continent, and I wish to add to this that I am an innocent man, have no connection whatever with this mystery as it is absolutely the work of someone else and not me.

I am eligible for parole and have the consideration of the Parole Committee which sits at this institution every three months, and I am asking you that if this story published in your magazine is true as to the characters and the incidents related in the story mentioned above, will you be so kind as to make affidavit to this effect, stating in it that the confession mentioned in the story is true?

Kind sir, you have no idea what or how much this will mean to me if same can be gotten. I have served 18 years for this crime, and I am as innocent of it as you are, and I verily believe that if you could do this, if it is a true confession, it will be the gate to my parole and release.

Yours respectfully,
[SIGNED] *Joseph Wendling*

The story Wendling referred to concerns the murder of Anna Aumuller by Father Hans Schmidt on September 2, 1913. That murder occurred in New York City. The two-part article about it was published in *True Detective Mysteries* magazine in the April and May 1928 issues.

As a result of his appeal, *True Detective Mysteries* launched an investigation, digging through the original records, "musty with age," and dispatching a seasoned local reporter to interview Wendling. *True Detective Mysteries* published a lengthy, two-part story about the Kellner murder in its March and April 1930 issues, written by a former *Courier-Journal* reporter, Mary Chenoweth. The article was entitled "The Crime Kentucky Can't Forget." It did not result, however, in any immediate change in Wendling's status.

In the many years since his conviction, Wendling had applied for clemency on at least ten occasions, with the most recent being placed before the state welfare board and Governor Ruby Laffoon.

Finally, in 1934, after twenty-three years, Frank Fehr withdrew his opposition to parole, provided that Wendling met two conditions: Wendling would have to make a full confession about the crime, and he would agree to deportation to France. It was revealed that Fehr had, in his possession, an eighteen-page letter written by Wendling in his own handwriting that implicated him in the crime, as an accessory, but not a complete confession. It had never been made public but had been used in the past to prevent Wendling from receiving parole since he first become eligible in 1919.

The warden at the Kentucky State Penitentiary at Eddyville, Tom Logan, reported that Wendling had a good record at the prison, where he had resided since the state transferred him there in 1921.

At long last, on January 25, 1935, Louisville learned that Joseph Wendling was to be paroled and deported. This news shared a headline with two other major events: the latest in the trial of Bruno Hauptmann, the alleged kidnapper and killer of the child of Charles Lindbergh; and the rescue of most of the passengers in the collision between the liner *Mohawk* and the freighter *Talisman* off the New Jersey shore. Wendling, it was reported, had completed his duties the evening before at the pumping station at the Eddyville Penitentiary, totally unaware that the parole he had been seeking for many years was on its way to Warden Logan. There were two conditions, but only one was made public—that he would be immediately deported to France.

It was expected that as soon as the papers reached the prison, the warden would arrange to start for New York with Wendling. There he would put him aboard a vessel bound for France. The state had obtained a passport from

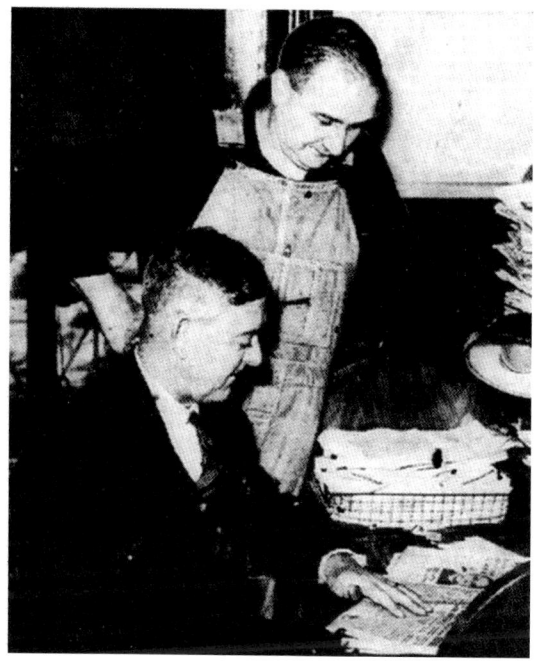

Joseph Wendling with warden Tom Logan as published in the *Courier-Journal*.

France and secured the tickets for his trip to New York and on to Europe. (It was assumed that Wendling's own funds, hoarded through years of prison work, were used, as the board had been assured that it would cost Kentucky nothing to deport him.)

The newspaper noted that Wendling had been a prisoner longer than "any other sane prisoner in the State's penal history." He was scheduled to leave on a liner departing on February 2, 1935. His destination was the little farm where his aged parents presumably still lived. Wendling claimed that his parents were about sixty-two, but it was noted that he could be mistaken, given his own age.

The newspaper reported the following:

> *The old prisoner radiated happiness with every movement early this morning when he stepped eagerly to Warden Logan's gray-walled office for perhaps his last full interview. The flush of joy and excitement somehow had banished the pallor of prison from his round face. He had just been told by the warden that "he was a free man at last." In the last interview, Wendling referred to the crime as "the case." He refused to say anything about Mr. Fehr other than to express his appreciation for what he had done for him and called him a "very fine man."*

Wendling, however, would leave Kentucky, and the United States, still carrying two secrets. The first was whether, in fact, he did murder Alma Kellner. The second was "what he wrote Frank Fehr, uncle of the girl, that caused Mr. Fehr to relent and recommend Wendling's parole to the Governor, subject, of course, to immediate deportation." He left the country with a few dollars in his pocket and about $100 that the prison had held from his work. In his time in prison, Wendling had become an expert electrician and machinist and for four years had operated the prison pumping station. He had previously operated the machine room. The newspaper reported that, "in one respect, safety of Eddyville's life and property has [been] depending on" Wendling, since the prison system also supplied water to the town of Eddyville. "When fire alarms rang, it was Wendling who, although behind a twenty-foot wall, stepped up the pressure and turned on an auxiliary pump" to aid firefighters in the town, whenever a fire was reported.

The warden, interviewed, noted: "Physically and mentally, Wendling has defied the natural disintegration of prison life. Warden Logan said ten years of imprisonment will drive an average man crazy, but Wendling is far from crazy. He is alert. He has kept up with current events, domestic and foreign, through the press and radio. He has read books on engineering and put his knowledge to practical use around the penitentiary. He is a self-taught radio technician, dismantled the first all-wave set he saw, then put it together again."

In a final interview before his departure, the reporter observed that Wendling's years in prison "have touched Wendling's shoulders only slightly. He is more erect than most men his age. His handclasp is firm and his weight of 200 pounds appears to be about normal. His black hair is graying at the temples only. There is no shuffle to his walk, no prison listlessness anywhere apparent." He had kept himself very well informed and "expressed anticipatory interest in seeing only two things—a talking picture and a dial telephone." He understood the "principle of the talking picture, but not of the dial." Wendling was reluctant to admit, in the presence of the warden, that he was anxious to leave the prison. Wendling expressed enjoyment of news radio programs and was looking forward to being a French farmer, although he expressed regret that he would "find himself among strangers at his old French home," as most of the men he would have known had died in the world war.

The reporters ended the interview by asking how Wendling had managed to survive his long incarceration in such good shape, mentally and physically.

He quickly responded: "Hope. I never lost hope, even for a second. I never gave up like I've seen 'em do. I knew that someday, somebody would do something to get me out of here. So I kept busy. I didn't eat enough to get a big belt. I obeyed the rules and never made trouble. I was always hopeful because I knew this would come some day, some way."

His departure from the prison was touching, according to the warden. He described Wendling as the "'old man' of the prison and everybody liked and respected him. Of course, all his friends among the convicts were glad to see him get out, but at the same time they were sorry to see him go."

The warden continued: "After a man has been in prison a few years he is always dreaming that he is a free man, only to wake up and find it a dream. That's what happened to Wendling. He knew, or thought he knew, that he was going to get out, but still it seemed too much like a dream to be true. But when his wife got there Sunday he broke down completely. After that, he realized it wasn't a dream."

On Tuesday, January 30, Wendling had a brief reunion in Louisville with friends who met his train at the Central Station. During his thirty-minute stopover between trains, he spent time with his wife, now seventy-five, and her brother Alois, with whom she lived. The old police chief, H. Watson Lindsey, now the sheriff, along with a detail of three deputies and Arnold's son Carl, shielded them from the curious stares of onlookers. Lena Wendling and her nephew had made the trip to the prison a few days before, on Sunday, for a last visit behind the privacy of the walls there. Wendling was dressed in a "dark blue suit, white shirt and blue and white polka dot bow tie." He seemed dazed, having last been through Louisville when he was transferred to Eddyville.

Technically, Wendling remained a prisoner, as the warden would not hand him his parole until he delivered Wendling to immigration and saw him safely aboard a ship for his ocean voyage. On his arrival in New York, he would have two days and three nights, staying at the Victoria Hotel, a brief opportunity to see some sights and in particular to see a sound moving picture. During his brief stay in New York with the warden and two Kentucky police officers, he went without handcuffs or shackles, as the warden trusted him. The warden declined the assistance of a guard in New York, and he and Wendling shared a room. When asked about his plans, Joseph Wendling stated that he would be returning to the family farm. He indicated that he had not heard from his parents there but assumed he would share the farm with them if they were still living, and if they were not, he would inherit it and work the farm himself.

On February 2, 1935, Joseph Wendling boarded a ship, the *Champlain*, heading to France. He noted that it was his fiftieth birthday on that day, despite prison records indicating that he was twelve years older. The warden accompanied Wendling to the ship and carried on the ship's manifest as a deportee. Wendling stayed in cabin No. 640, and his passage cost about $125, which Wendling paid for out of money he had saved from the sale of trinkets and his radio repair work.

However, Wendling's departure did not end the story. It was rumored that Wendling had stated that the Kellner family had offered him 250,000 francs (approximately $16,500) as an indemnity for his unlawful detention. Frank Fehr, however, denied that absolutely.

In Paris, a different version of the tale was told with the story of Joseph-Henry Wendling, "an 'etonnante histoire'—an astonishing tale" as reported in *Paris Soir*, a French newspaper. A dramatic headline in the *Louisville Magazine*, a satellite publication of the *Courier-Journal*, stated, "Louisville's Church Cellar Fiend Becomes a Martyr in France"—"an 'innocent Frenchman' who was the persecuted victim of an American mistake." A full-page article reported the "tear-jerking story," stating that it was the confession of the true murderer that resulted in his release, with Wendling the "innocent Frenchman." In an amusing error, the French article described the governor as "Monsieur Rugby Lafon, governor of the national prison of the State of Kentucky, the prison of Francfort at Eddyville." The governor at the time was Ruby Laffoon, and of course, Kentucky is a state, with a prison in both Frankfort and Eddyville. Wendling had been given 500,000 francs by the government (Kentucky) and 250,000 francs by the Kellners, an amount totaling approximately $50,000. The remaining story was rife with errors, a complete fabrication. The horrors of prison were detailed, and the devotion of Wendling to his wife, named Henriette Jacquemin, was described, even though "they were divorced by the American law forbidding a woman to remain the wife of a convict for life." Wendling claimed that, despite their long separation, they were still "united before God." He was described as having reached Genlis and visited the graves of his deceased parents—likely the only true information in the entire article.

The *Courier-Journal* reviewed the case and noted that, of course, the report of any payment to Joseph Wendling was news to the Kellner-Fehr family and to former governor Laffoon.

Lena Wendling joined the frenzy of litigation, filing a lawsuit against Herman Morris for failing to secure the release of her husband. She had hired Morris when he promised to do so, claiming to have the "means or information by which he could get Wendling released from the penitentiary." She had borrowed $750.00 from her brother and others. When nothing was done, she demanded the return of the money, and he gave her a check for $807.50, the original amount plus interest. However, the bank from which it was drawn informed her that there were no funds in the account. When Morris did not respond to the lawsuit, she obtained judgement by default, but it seems unlikely she ever recovered on the matter.

15

THE PRIEST

The question, of course, is, was Joseph Wendling guilty? He publicly maintained his innocence throughout his trial, appeals, incarceration and pardon and until he left the United States and returned to France. At the time he was charged, he was the obvious suspect. Nevertheless, a few years later, an alternative suspect appeared in a dramatic fashion.

In September 1913, police found a woman's mutilated body in the East River in New York City. The investigation quickly focused on one Hans Schmidt, a Catholic priest. He quickly confessed to the murder of the young woman, Anna Aumuller, whom he had married. It was soon learned, and publicized in Louisville, that from the summer of 1909 until April 1910, Father Schmidt, a German national, had resided with Father B. Henry Westermann, the pastor of the Church of the Immaculate Conception, located at Eighth and Grayson streets in Louisville. He had been sent to the parish by Bishop McCloskey to improve his English in order to take on the role of an active priest in the United States.

The mode of the New York murder was telling. Schmidt confessed to slitting his young bride's throat, cutting her into nine pieces, bundling up the parts into five packages and dumping them into the water from a Weehawken ferryboat. In his confession, he claimed that he was commanded to sacrifice her by his patron saint, St. Elizabeth of Hungary. He drank some of her blood to consummate the sacrifice. At the time of the murder, the couple had been married for some six months. They had obtained a marriage license, and Schmidt had performed the ceremony himself.

A few weeks later, Schmidt was still professing his guilt and expressing his willingness to die in the electric chair. He also "declared that if he could convince the Louisville authorities that he was guilty of the murder of little Alma Kellner, who met her death while he was connected with St. John's church in that city, he would gladly confess that crime and thus save John Wendling, the former school janitor, who is now serving a life term at Frankfort for the murder." However, in other interviews, he maintained his innocence in that murder, stating that if he had done it, he "would gladly confess all."

The newspaper noted that "eight alienists, otherwise known as insanity experts," were employed in the case. His first trial, during which he professed insanity, resulted in a mistrial. His retrial was first scheduled for January 12, 1914, and then moved to February 4, 1914. He was promptly convicted and sentenced to die the next month. Schmidt received a stay based on his appeal, using the argument that, in fact, his wife had died during an illegal abortion. His appeal was unsuccessful, however, and Governor Charles S. Whitman refused to further delay his execution. Although pressed at the end by his priest confessor about the death of Alma Kellner, he denied emphatically having been involved in that crime.

On February 18, he became the first and, as of yet, the only Catholic priest to be executed in the United States, when he went to his death in the electric chair in Sing Sing Prison in New York.

Epilogue

Following the Joseph Wendling trial, life moved on. In the course of time, the lives of those involved in the Alma Kellner murder case ended.

In December 1910, the newspaper reported that the "scramble for the rewards" offered by various parties concerning the Wendling prosecution was expected to start with the filing of lawsuits. With so many claims, it seemed inevitable. Cora Munea, of course, was one, but many others put in claims for all or part of the rewards, as well.

In July 1911, George Ellis filed multiple lawsuits in two different courts. He was making a claim to the various rewards, naming as defendants, and the amounts, as follows:

City of Louisville, $2,500.00
John H. and James P. Whallen, $1,000.00
Fred F. Kellner, $1,000.00
Central Consumers Company, $1,000.00
Frank Fehr, $1,000.00
Louisville Courier-Journal Company and Times Company, $1,000.00
Louisville Times Company (as trustee), $102.99
Vic Lorch, $50.00
Charles Dehler, $100.00

Epilogue

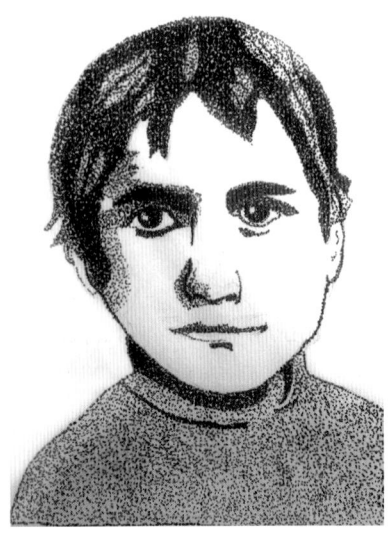

Alma Kellner, original illustration by Melanie Hilliard.

Ellis claimed that his information had been "primarily, chiefly and principally responsible" for Wendling's ultimate capture and that he was entitled to all of the available reward money. Several others made claims: Cora Munea, Thomas F. Burke, George Ryan and R. McAnally, the latter having provided the street address for Wendling in San Francisco to the San Francisco police chief.

The lawsuit dragged on for several years. In May 1914, Judge James Quarles awarded 60 percent of the reward to McAnally, the other 40 percent to be divided between Burke and Ryan. However, Ellis had entered into an agreement with those three parties to share any reward received. Cora Munea was not included, and some of the funds were held back should her claim go forward, although it is unclear if she ever, in fact, received any money. It was noted that "the expenses have been so heavy that comparatively little will go to the victors." The City of Louisville, in addition, refused to pay the reward it had offered, arguing that it was illegal for the city to have offered it in the first place.

R.B. Sweet, the plumber who found the body of Alma Kellner, filed suit in January 1915 against James P. Whallen, the surviving member of the Whallen firm, claiming the $500 reward that had been offered for information leading to the discovery of the child. Judges Quarles had settled other disputes the previous year. It is unclear whether Sweet ever received any of the reward he claimed. Sweet passed away in 1923 and was laid to rest in Eastern Cemetery in Louisville.

St. John's Catholic Church, while still standing, is no longer a consecrated Catholic church. Built initially as a place for Catholic immigrants, primarily the Germans who lived in that area, it was eventually de-consecrated as a church when demographics changed. It became, and still is, a haven for men needing assistance and is known as the St. John Center for Homeless Men. Although the pews have been removed and the interior of the church is used as administrative offices, the beautiful altar and vivid stained-glass windows of a church of that era remain. The rectory and other buildings from 1909 no longer stand on the property. The Kellner home on Broadway also no longer exists, but the family's later home, a substantial brick structure at 703 Rubel avenue, is located right off Broadway. The train station where Wendling arrived after the manhunt, now called Union Station, still serves as a transportation hub for Louisville, but for the Transit Authority of River City (TARC), the municipal bus company, rather than for passenger trains. The Frankfort penitentiary was demolished after the devastating 1937 flood, but the Kentucky State Penitentiary at Eddyville, known as "The Castle," still serves as the primary penitentiary for the Commonwealth of Kentucky.

As was the norm, the newspaper reported the comings and goings of well-known members of Louisville society. In 1912, it was reported that Miss Elizabeth Weitzel had come from Frankfort to spend the winter with her sister's family. In July 1914, Minnie and young Frederick, along with their aunt, Elizabeth Weitzel, paid a visit of several weeks to Elizabeth and Florence's sister-in-law, Mrs. William Weitzel. Florence Kellner returned in November from a visit with her sisters, Mrs. William Weitzel and Mrs. William Mandeville. In 1915, another sister, Margaretta, also paid a visit. Elizabeth Weitzel lived with her sister and brother-in-law on and off for many years, never marrying. She passed away in Frankfort, Kentucky, in November 1943 and is interred in Frankfort Cemetery.

On May 9, 1917, the Kellner family suffered another tragedy when Minnie Weitzel Kellner, age seventeen, passed away from heart disease. She was buried following a service at St. Boniface Church and was laid next to her younger sister in St. Louis Cemetery.

Joseph Wendling's long-devoted wife lived out her life with her brother Alois. Alois Arnold had become a widower in 1902, leaving him with three young children. In June 1918, following the end of World War I, German alien women were required to register. One of the women who did so on the first day was "Mary Madeline [*sic*] Wendling," Joseph Wendling's wife, who lived at 1528 Garland avenue. Despite the years that had passed, the first line mentioned her connection to the murder. Lena Wendling predeceased her brother by less than a year and died on September 6, 1952. She, like her brother, was buried in Calvary Cemetery in Louisville. Her death certificate and her grave marker indicated that she was single and gave her surname not as Wendling but as Arnold.

Captain John Carney, who was originally from Buffalo, New York, and served for a time with the Chicago Police Department as well as with the Pinkerton Detective Agency, the Lake Shore Railroad and the South Bend,

Epilogue

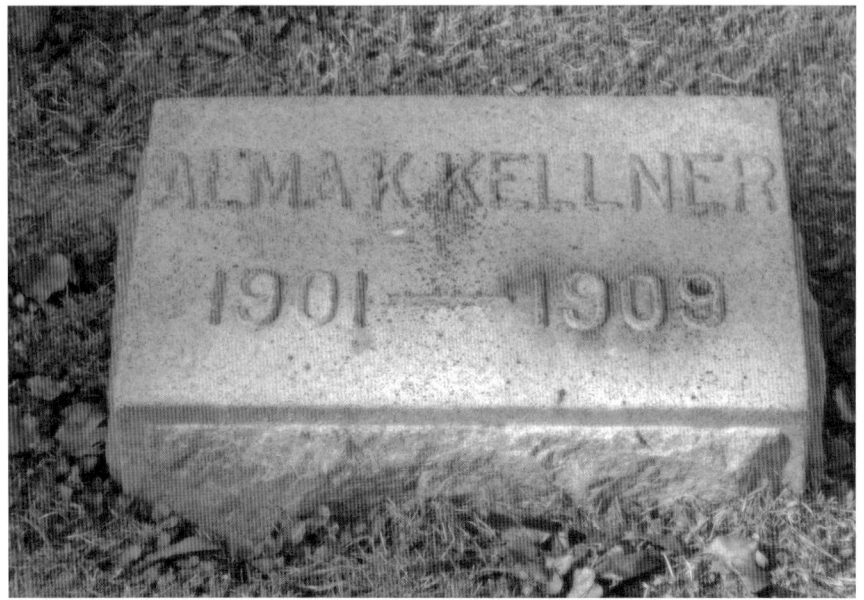

Gravestone of Alma Kellner, St. Louis Cemetery, Louisville, Kentucky. *Photo by author.*

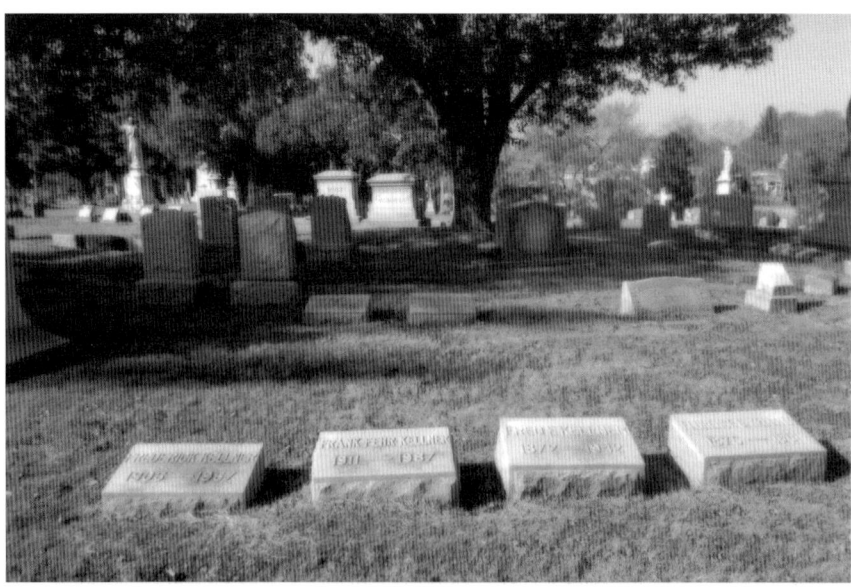

Cemetery plot containing the graves of Alma and Minnie Kellner (*in the rear*) and Frederick Jr., Frank Fehr, Frederick Sr. and Florence Kellner (*in the front*). *Photo by author.*

Epilogue

Indiana police, eventually resigned from the Louisville Police Department and returned to New York. He passed away suddenly in 1927 in Saratoga Springs, New York, at the age of fifty-nine while again working for the Pinkertons.

Frederick Kellner passed away in 1942, followed by his wife, Florence Weitzel Kellner, in 1961. They were survived by their two sons, John Frederick and Frank Fehr. They lived at the home on Rubel avenue until their deaths and remained members of St. Boniface Parish. They lie together in the St. Louis Cemetery in Louisville, Kentucky, in the same plot where Alma and Minnie are interred.

John Frederick Kellner was three years old at the time of his sister's death. In 1922, he was among hundreds of other children who qualified to win a ticket for a performance at the National Theater. He was not one of the sixteen capital prizewinners, however, who received baseball outfits (for the boys) and ball-bearing roller skates (for the girls). Six other children received the Booth Tarkington "Penrod" storybooks. The contest involved solving a scrambled "face" puzzle, that of the face of Wesley Barry, a young motion picture star. At the time, the news reported that he lived at 703 Rubel avenue with his family. He died in 1967 and was also laid to rest with his family. His wife, Mildred, who survived him by many years, is buried elsewhere. He had no children at the time of his death.

The Reverend George William Schuhmann, later a monsignor, remained a priest until his death on November 29, 1931. His funeral was held at St. John's Catholic Church, which he had faithfully served for twenty-five years. He was a well-respected parish priest throughout his life. At the time of his death, he was the vicar general of the diocese. In his memory, the Schuhmann Social Service Center connected with St. Martin de Tours Parish was named for him. It opened in 1982 to provide aid to the homeless and those in need in the community. He lies at rest in St. Louis Cemetery, next to Bishop Denis O'Donaghue, whom he served, and not far from Alma Kellner and her family.

Chief Henry Watson Lindsey died on November 23, 1943, having served as Louisville's police chief from 1909 to 1917. He is buried in Frankfort Cemetery.

Frank Fehr died in 1962 after holding the position of president of the brewery for many years. Although his obituary detailed his long life and many interests in Louisville, nothing was mentioned of the Kellner case. Fehr Road in Louisville is named for his family. His namesake, Frank Fehr Kellner, called Fehr, was born to the Kellners the year following his sister's

Epilogue

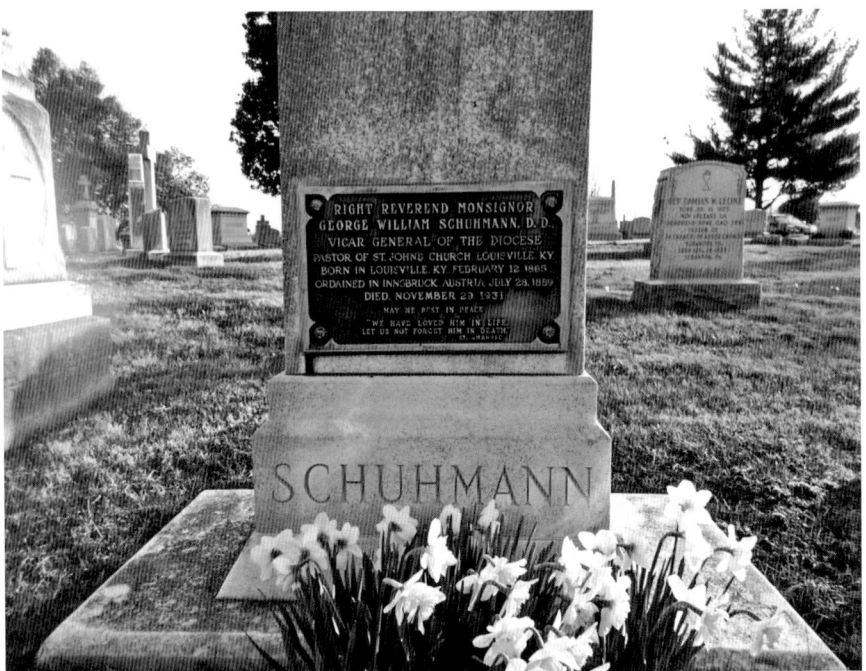

Grave marker for Father William Schuhmann, St. Louis Cemetery. *Photo by author.*

murder. He married Dorothy Grewling and had several children and worked as a radio technician. He died in Florida in 1987, and his body was returned to Louisville. He was buried with the rest of his family and lies at the foot of the grave of the sister he never knew.

Joseph Wendling, it can only be presumed, died in France, taking the secret of his guilt or innocence to his grave.

Notes

Chapter 1

1. In the style of the time, "street" was normally lowercased in newspaper stories.
2. The school was also called St. Mary's School in some stories. The school eventually became only a high school; for a brief time, it included a junior high in the 1970s. The school relocated in 2007, and the building on Broadway was razed in 2016. Coincidentally, the author is a proud 1977 graduate of the Academy of Our Lady of Mercy, entering for six years through the same door that Alma Kellner would have used during her time as a student.

Chapter 3

3. Mrs. Wendling was known by several variations of her name—Mary Magdalena, Magdalena, Lena and even Madeline.

Chapter 4

4. Some references state that her family lived in Alsace, France, the area straddling the border of the two countries.
5. St. Peter's Catholic Church was razed in 1973.

Notes

Chapter 5

6. In fact, Kentucky law still provides for such a reward for the apprehension and return of a fugitive from justice. Although the current publication states that the law dates from 1942, that is when a major recodification of Kentucky law occurred. In fact, the statutes in place now are identical to those in place in 1910; they simply carry a different statute number. The statutes, as they are now, read as follows:

   > *KRS 446.100 Reward for apprehension of fugitive from justice. In aggravated cases of murder and other felonies against the person when the accused flees from justice, the Governor, on petition of the Circuit or District Judge of the county, may issue a proclamation offering a reward of not more than five hundred dollars ($500) for the apprehension of the accused. This reward shall be paid upon production of a receipt from the officer named in the Governor's proclamation, showing delivery of the fugitive to him, approved and certified by the Circuit Court of the county of that officer's residence*

   > *440.110 Proclamation offering reward—Publication.*
   > *(1) Whenever the Governor issues a proclamation offering a reward for a fugitive from justice or anyone charged with crime, he shall designate in his proclamation the jail to which the prisoner shall be delivered. It need not be the jail of the county where the offense was committed. (2) The Governor may order the proclamation published in a newspaper if he deems it proper under the circumstances and to the interest of the state. If he orders it published, he shall designate the paper or papers in which the publication shall be made and the number of times it shall be inserted. The account for such publication, with the approval of the Governor endorsed on it, shall be paid out of the State Treasury.*

7. Sweating—intense questioning under physical or emotional duress—was a common practice at the time, but it was prohibited by a state law passed in 1912. During an attempt in 1916 to repeal it, Chief Lindsey stated that "sweating prisoners is an antiquated form of police work that no efficient and fair-minded police official will use." He stated at that time that he would "not allow any member of the Louisville police force to browbeat, cuff or abuse a prisoner so long as I am in command." The law against such use of the "third degree" continues today in the following statute:

Notes

422.110 Obtaining confessions by "sweating" prohibited.
No peace officer, or other person having lawful custody of any person charged with crime, shall attempt to obtain information from the accused concerning his connection with or knowledge of crime by plying him with questions, or extort information to be used against him on his trial by threats or other wrongful means, nor shall the person having custody of the accused permit any other person to do so.

The penalty for violation of the statute, found in KRS 422.990, is a fine of between $100 and $500 or jail of between ten and sixty days, or both, making it a misdemeanor.

Chapter 7

8. This was not a title but, apparently, his actual name.
9. Although the newspaper account indicates June, this was undoubtedly actually written in July.
10. The Bertillon system of criminal investigation was in use during this time. It was based on the belief that each individual had a "unique combination of measurements of different body parts," such as the skull and the ears, and that such measurements could be used to identify an individual.
11. A "yeggman" was a safecracker or burglar.
12. At the time, Louisville had a bicameral legislative branch, with the general council sitting as the lower body and the board of alderman as the upper body.

Chapter 9

13. This route would seem odd to a modern citizen of Louisville, as Jefferson street is now one-way westbound.
14. As Alois Arnold's deceased wife was Mary Anna Kippes, it can be presumed that this individual was perhaps a brother-in-law.

Notes

Chapter 10

15. The jail building in use at the time is now known as the "Old Jail" and is used for court-related purposes.

Chapter 11

16. The newspaper account provided full addresses for each, as it was not expected that trial jurors would be anonymous. In addition, no alternate jurors were seated, as would be expected today in a trial of such magnitude. In consideration of the privacy of possible current occupants of any existing houses, the full address is not given for any house that is still standing.
17. At the time, blackboards were often made from a combination of lime, plaster of Paris and lampblack.
18. Both the rectory and the old school building are now gone, replaced by a single, modern building that fills the entire space.

Chapter 12

19. This requirement exists today and is referred to as the "Corroboration Rule" in the Kentucky Rules of Criminal Procedure, Rule 9.60, Corroboration of confession. It reads: "A confession of a defendant, unless made in open court, will not warrant a conviction unless accompanied by other proof that such an offense was committed."

Chapter 13

20. Kentucky's Old Capitol Building was supplanted by the New Capitol that exists today. The New Capitol was being dedicated at the same time the manhunt for Joseph Wendling started. The Old Capitol is now designated as a U.S. National Historic Landmark and serves as a museum and the home of the Kentucky Historical Society. It was also the site of the only governor to be assassinated, Governor-Elect William Goebel, who was walking into the capitol when he was shot from an adjacent building. Having worked through an election contest, Goebel was sworn in on his deathbed.

Bibliography

Advocate-Messenger (Danville, KY). "Joseph Wendling, Poet." August 18, 1911, 7.

Central Record (Lancaster, KY). "Body of Alma Kellner Found." June 3, 1910, 1.

Chenoweth, Mary. "The Crime Kentucky Can't Forget." *True Detective Mysteries* (March–April 1930).

Commonwealth v. Wendling, Jefferson Circuit Court, November 28–December 3, 1910.

Commonwealth v. Wendling, 182 F. 140 (W.D. Ky., 1910).

Courier-Journal (Louisville, KY). "Another Suspect." June 6, 1910, 2.

———. "Asks Part of Reward." August 7, 1910, 3.

———. "Begin Taking the Testimony To-Day." November 30, 1910, 1.

———. "Benedict Thomas Has a Good Alibi." July 31, 1910, 4

———. "Carney Gives Attorney Clements the Slip." August 12, 1910, 1.

———. "Carney Leaves with Wendling." August 11, 1910, 1.

———. "Carney Will Start To-Day." August 9, 1910, 1.

———. "Chief Carney Ill." August 7, 1910, 3.

———. "Chief Carney Still Working in Texas." June 25, 1910, 3.

———. "Chief Ellis." August 17, 1910, 2.

———. "Claims Reward." July 14, 1911, 10.

———. "Col. J.P. Whallen Met Carney in Frisco." July 31, 1910, 5.

———. "Col. Lindsey Back from Denver, Col." August 9, 1910, 2.

———. "Consular Aid Sought for Wendling Parole." July 14, 1922, 3.

Bibliography

———. "Coroner to Conduct an Inquest Soon." June 3, 1910, 2.

———. "Crime Laid at Wendling's Door." June 10, 1910, 1.

———. "Crippen and Girl Arrested." August 1, 1910, 1.

———. "Detectives Think They Know Who Killed Alma Kellner." May 30, 1910, 1.

———. "Did Not Look Where Body Was." August 6, 1910, 2.

———. "Divides Reward." May 31, 1914, 8.

———. "Drag-net Is World-Wide." June 3, 1910, 1.

———. "Eight-year Old Girl Is Missing." December 9, 1909, 1.

———. "Fails in Effort to Have Woman Released." June 3, 1910, 2.

———. "Father Van De Pritte Makes No Comment." July 31, 1910, 4.

———. "Five Jurors Have Been Agreed Upon." November 29, 1910, 1.

———. "Former Head of Detectives Dies." September 4, 1927, 1.

———. "Frisco Detective Will Testify in Wendling Case." November 20, 1910, 47.

———. "Get the Testimony." November 17, 1910, 5.

———. "Girl Bears Word to Mother from Kidnapers." December 10, 1909, 1.

———. "Girl Medium Fails to Throw Light on Disappearance of Alma Kellner." December 15, 1909, 8.

———. "Governor Willson Offers a Reward of $500." June 3, 1910, 2.

———. "Habeas Corpus Proceedings." August 10, 1910, 1.

———. "Here to Testify in the Wendling Case." November 27, 1910, 11.

———. "Hold Inquest This Morning." June 8, 1910, 1.

———. "In a Stateroom of a Pullman." August 7, 1910, 1.

———. "Janitor's Wife Is Becoming Resigned." June 3, 1910, 2.

———. "'Japs' Have Wendling Suspect Shadowed." September 10, 1910.

———. "Judge Directs Jury to Probe Social Unrest." September 2, 1919, 5.

———. "Judge Evans Has Wendling Case Under Submission." October 20, 1910, 3.

———. "Leaves 'Frisco with a Smile." August 3, 1910, 1.

———. "Light Sentence." November 15, 1910, 10.

———. "Lindsey Obtains Little from the Prisoner." August 7, 1910, 1.

———. "More Money." September 7, 1910, 2

———. "Mrs. Joseph Wendling Sues Attorney for $807.50." January 22, 1913, 12.

———. "New Lawyer for Wending." October 4, 1911, 2.

———. "No Word from Alma Kellner." December 11, 1909, 1

———. "On the Lookout." June 6, 1910, 2.

———. "On the Trail of the Suspect." June 22, 1910, 1.

Bibliography

———. "Parents Grieve, Kentucky Irish American." December 11, 1909, 4.
———. "Parents Unable to Attend the Funeral." June 1, 1910, 1.
———. "Physicians Found." August 17, 1910, 2.
———. "Plumber Sues for Reward." January 9, 1915, 3.
———. "Police Advance New Theory." June 5, 1910, 31.
———. "Police Make Long Run in Automobile." June 6, 1910, 2.
———. "Police Still Have a Hope." February 15, 1909, 1.
———. "Prisoner Not Joe Wendling." June 6, 1910, 1.
———. "Progress Slow." February 28, 1913, 12.
———. "Ralph Campbell Now on Trial." November 22, 1910, 5.
———. "Reports on Year's Work of Police." September 23, 1910, 10.
———. "Reward Claim." January 9, 1914, 5.
———. "Rites Held for Vicar General." December 3, 1931, 9.
———. "Rumor of His Escape Surprise to Wendling." December 10, 1915, 10.
———. "Secretary of War Enlisted in Search." June 3, 1910, 2.
———. "Shovel Used for Digging Girl's Grave." June 3, 1910, 2.
———. "Stains from Human Blood." June 4, 1910, 1.
———. "Stains Said to Be from Human Blood." June 3, 1910, 2.
———. "$10,000 Reward for Murderer." June 2, 1910, 1.
———. "Testimonial." August 6, 1910, 12.
———. "'Thank God!' Wendling's Cry." August 6, 1910, 2.
———. "Thorne Still Trying, but Just Can't Escape." April 20, 1918, 14.
———. "Thought Her Husband Had Gone to Europe." June 3, 1910, 2.
———. "Tom Logan Trusts Wendling, He Says." January 31, 1935, 1.
———. "To Prosecute to Full Extent of Law." July 31, 1910, 4.
———. "To State Courts." October 21, 1910, 10.
———. "Tried to Sell Wendling's Pictures." September 6, 1910, 10.
———. "Trout, Allan M., Wendling Happy Now." January 26, 1935, 1.
———. "$200 Reward Will Be Paid for Wendling." August 23, 1919, 1.
———. "Wendling Believed to Be in Italy." July 27, 1910, 1.
———. "Wendling Breaks Down and Weeps." December 1, 1910, 1.
———. "Wendling Case Up." March 16, 1911, 5.
———. "Wendling Fled after Trap Laid for Girl Failed." August 24, 1919, 1
———. "Wendling Had No Callers Today." August, 15, 1910, 10.
———. "Wendling Has Few Visitors." August 14, 1910, 32.
———. "Wendling Held in St. Louis Faced by Mrs. Munea." August 8, 1910, 1.

ABOUT THE AUTHOR

Shawn M. Herron is a lifelong resident of Louisville, Kentucky, and can count back five generations of family members who proudly called the city home. Shawn holds a BA in English from the University of Louisville and a JD from the Brandeis School of Law. She has been practicing in the area of public safety law for over twenty-five years. She has worked for the *Courier-Journal*, the City of Louisville, the Jefferson County Sheriff's Office and, now, the Kentucky Department of Criminal Justice Training, where she trains law enforcement officers. An inveterate and omnivorous reader, Shawn maintains a blog called Kentucky Cop Stories and is a regular contributor to the *Kentucky Law Enforcement* magazine. She has also contributed articles to *Police Chief* and *Sheriff* magazines. Shawn also serves as the volunteer search and rescue coordinator for the Louisville Metro Emergency Management Agency and is a member of the Madison County Rescue Squad. Shawn is a member of the Louisville Historical League and the Filson Club, both of which showcase local history. She lives in a house that is more than 150 years old in Portland with several cats.

Visit us at
www.historypress.net